HOLY WIND

HOLY FIRE

Finding Your Vibrant Spirit

through Scripture

PAMELA A. SMITH, SS.C.M.

all the best to you!

Pamela Smith, SSCM

TWENTY-THIRD
PUBLICATIONS
twentythirdpublications.com

TWENTY-THIRD PUBLICATIONS
One Montauk Avenue, Suite 200
New London, CT 06320
(860) 437-3012 or (800) 321-0411
www.twentythirdpublications.com

ISBN: 978-1-62785-317-0
Library of Congress Control Number: 2017944487
Printed in the U.S.A.

A division of Bayard, Inc.

DEDICATED TO

MICHAEL DENNIS BROWNE
at "Poetry, Prose, and Prayer,"
Collegeville Institute for Ecumenical
and Cultural Research, MN, 2015

THE STAFF AND WRITERS-IN-RESIDENCE
at Weymouth Center for the Arts and Humanities
and **THE PARISHIONERS, ADORERS, AND CLERGY**
at St. Anthony of Padua Church,
Southern Pines, NC, 2016

THE CHILDREN OF LIGHT
at Lourdes Regional, Shamokin, PA 1972-1973

and, of course,
THE SISTERS OF SS. CYRIL AND METHODIUS,
companions on the journey for 45 years

CONTENTS

SELECTED NEW TESTAMENT READINGS

INTRODUCTION

We want energy, vitality, enthusiasm, vigor, pizzazz—and we want these everywhere.

At home, we get into a happy dither when the new baby arrives, when company is coming, when it's time for a party, when we're about to embark on a long-awaited vacation, when we're redecorating, when the garden blooms lavishly, when the sweepstakes tribe stands at the door dazzling us with cameras and the super-sized check in hand. At school, we mark "spirit days" with school colors ablaze, special shirts, pep rallies, and all kinds of breaks from schedules and routine. At work, we stir things up when there's an unexpected promotion or raise, when there's an office party, and when a new venture is launched, complete with banners and balloons.

At church, we sing, sway, and praise when there's spirited preaching, moving music, gifted leadership, color, ambiance, friendly greetings, the grand finale to capital campaigns, a wow of a retreat or parish mission, and reassurances of saving grace.

What we don't want, what we truly dread, is boredom, apathy, lethargy, ennui, sadness. We don't want a depression that droops out of bed and persists as we drag through the day. We don't want Mopey-Joe companions and rooms full of blahs.

So, along with the spirit that puts our feet on the floor in the morning and ignites the engine that thrusts us gladly into the day, we want

Spirit—the Holy Spirit who is, by nature and definition, life and love. We want a Spirit who is over, under, around, and through all that we consider thrilling but also all that we consider routine. We want something, Someone, who gives us purpose, passion, and perseverance. We want a Spirit who is here-and-now yet also somewhere else, perceptible but mysterious, simultaneously within and larger than our lives. And we want that Spirit to overwhelm us and everyone else with get-up-and-go that gladdens us and makes sense of our lives.

In church circles, we call this Holy Spirit the one who dwells in us and is the source of our inspirations and good impulses. We call this Spirit the bond of God, Father and Son, Creator and Redeemer. We name the Holy Spirit "Lord and giver of life" in our creed. And we claim, in the words of the sainted pope many call Great, that "personal love *is* the Holy Spirit" (John Paul II, *Dominum et Vivificantem*).

If this Spirit is, deep down, the one we want and claim, we can expect to be living confidently, vibrantly, resolutely. If somehow we are not quite living vivaciously, we may need some reminders of who the Holy Spirit is and how this Spirit enlivens. Thus, this book offers a journey through Scriptures that tell how verve and zip arise in the first place and how the Spirit can be counted on to make a comeback when we find ourselves amid dispirited days.

Selected

OLD

TESTAMENT

Readings

1 | IN THE BEGINNING

≋ READ GENESIS 1:1—2:3

In the beginning when God created the heavens and the earth, the earth was a formless void and darkness covered the face of the deep, while a wind from God swept over the face of the waters. GENESIS 1:1–2

The Holy Spirit begins at the beginning, making of what *is not* a multitude of what *is*. The Spirit comes as a mighty wind, spiraling a murky waste into pulsing crests and troughs. Mountains, valleys, river beds, deserts, prairies, waterfalls, ocean waves, gritty beaches all come to be. The wind of the Spirit rotates until we stop spinning. Grasses sprout, pines launch, and dwarf palmettos cluster and huddle in the sudden humidity. Amoebas lead a procession into complexity, and fins stir, frogs splash and leap ashore, lizards crawl, birds chirp, and furry hides fend off buzzing insects. We wake and sleep and wake again.

The Spirit, of course, is before all this birthing and beyond all that we call universe. Since we live in that creation called time, we cannot fathom what eternity, neither frontward nor backward, might mean. Eternity is every direction and always now. There are, astronomers tell us, billions of star systems in the known universe. There are, biologists tell us, a plethora of strange and wondrous living species on planet Earth. All of them, we believe, are Spirit-birthed and Spirit-work, swathed in a Spirit who is everywhere, elsewhere, all at once, here, active, present, heretofore, and future too. What we see are the beauty marks of divinity.

The wind, Scripture says, is "mighty." God breezes and breathes, sometimes bellowing, over all that we have ever heard of and know. When flags flap or sails billow, when the whisks of autumn scatter leaves and muss our hair, we might remember.

The Spirit is manifest as maker of magnificence.

And so worship begins as morning breaks and a bluebird lights on the swing in a dewy yard.

Dawn on me, O Spirit, and stir a breeze that remembers beauty, variety, and grace. Let me always be thankful for lily pads flowering white and pink, rippling ponds, woodpeckers knocking on sleeping trees, raccoons that work nocturnal banditry, and also for scruffy truckers and women who cartwheel when they're ninety.

≡ **FOR REFLECTION**

- If I have toured a cave or an inactive mine and stood still at that moment when the guide turned out the lights, did I get a bit of insight into what that first nothingness might have been like? How was it when the lights came on? Can I imagine the wonder of the first conscious beings?

- Have I considered how many religious people—including clerics like Copernicus, Mendel, Steno (geology), Chardin, and others—have contributed to our understanding of the natural world? How do I deal with the supposed conflict between science and religion?

- Archbishop Luis Martinez called the Holy Spirit "the Artist of souls" (*True Devotion*, 11). When am I most likely to see the variety of the natural world and of humanity as artistry? Do I sense that the continuum of creation is a soulful work?

2 | BREATH OF LIFE

READ GENESIS 2:4–25

Then the Lord God formed man from the dust of the ground, and breathed into his nostrils the breath of life; and the man became a living being. GENESIS 2:7

The same Hebrew word, *ru'ah*, translates as "wind," "breath," and "spirit." There is no question that the chosen people had a profound sense that God's Spirit was the origin of all creation, of respiration, and of that ineffable life-force that orients us toward transcendence. Living on planet Earth means that we arrive amid hubbub and are propelled forward—to life and to eternity.

At that primeval moment when humanity came to be distinct from other beings, we were capable of reason, goodness, equanimity, and gratitude. We found ourselves comfortable with solitude and solidarity, and we grasped the importance of communion with both creatures and the Creator. Then things fractured and fell.

Despite the evidence all around us of our species' potential for selfishness, sin, and crime, we must admit that human beings are remarkable specimens. We have gradually learned to navigate the natural world and function within the smaller and larger circles in which we have found ourselves. We have formed friendships and alliances, fallen in love, and generated families. We have imagined and adapted and researched and invented. We have formed institutions that advance learning and culture and athletic prowess and the arts, and we have decorated both ourselves and our surroundings with color and class. We number among our ancestral tribes and nations a vast collection of saints, geniuses, and heroes.

Male and female, we have the potential to be such, too. We, like the first of our forebears, are invited to be, to breathe, to gather around the tree of life.

We pause to inhale deeply and know that we are, in some supernatural way, drawing in not merely air but the breath of God.

⫸ **PRAYER**

God of life and breath, let me choose to celebrate the goodness of being here and being now. Teach me to live the fullness of the potential with which you have endowed me.

⫸ **FOR REFLECTION**

- Do I ever stop to think about my heartbeat and breathing as something other than a medical concern—but instead as a mystery of the universe? What helps me tune into the Spirit-filled aspect of the rhythms of my living?

- If I have witnessed the birth of a child, how did I feel and what did I think when the baby took that first breath? Did I sense something of godliness in that moment?

3 | THE DOVE

🕊 **READ GENESIS 8:6–19**

He waited another seven days…; and the dove came back to him in the evening, and there in its beak was a freshly plucked olive leaf.

GENESIS 8:10–11

The dove is the classic symbol of the Holy Spirit, from its association with Noah's testing the waters for emergence from the ark, to its appearance at the baptism of the Lord. We use the dove with the olive branch as a symbol of peace.

Perhaps it is the whiteness of the dove that signals life and hope to us. Perhaps it is the gentle cooing that seems almost to mother and lullaby us. Perhaps it is the dove's easy glide and its comfortable closeness that relax us. Perhaps it is the dove's hovering that suggests that we are watched over and cooled from the heat.

The dove is a fine reminder of safety and serenity. The murmuring dove offers serene overshadowing and attention. We expect the Spirit to carry greenery to us, in a homing beak.

🕊 **PRAYER**

Spirit of peace, come to me with signs of life. I long for homecoming and need you to re-inhabit me. Along with our whole world, I long for respite, peace, and renewal.

🕊 **FOR REFLECTION**

- A world of terrorism and societal violence needs peace. What signs and symbols bring me a sense of relief? What restores my confidence in civil society?

- Where does my own homing spirit lead? How is the place where I feel most at home both memorable and always new to me?

4 | THE BURNING BUSH

READ EXODUS 3:1-14

Moses led his flock beyond the wilderness, and came to Horeb, the mountain of God. There the angel of the Lord appeared to him in a flame of fire out of a bush; he looked, and the bush was blazing, yet it was not consumed. EXODUS 3:1B–2

At first blush, "I AM" seems a strange name for God. Yet that is exactly, and paradoxically, the name God claims. Philosophers and theologians have described God as pure being, first cause, prime mover, source and sum of all that is. Being itself, *personal* being, is God's identity. And, of course, being an "I" implies that there is some "you" to whom one relates.

What we sometimes don't get, when we consider Moses' shoeless encounter with God on holy ground, is that this Spirit God is otherworldly and yet also visible (in fire) and audible (in speech). This God confounds normal expectations but clearly wants to get something across: to make things happen, to help people notice. God sends Moses on a mission, assuredly, but more important than that, God wants people to grasp the fact that their God is near, attentive, moved by their need and grief, and available to be known. As the march out of Egypt begins and continues, the cloud and pillar of fire become the sign of God's ongoing presence.

Unbeknownst to them, the whole Trinity is present. Light, Life, and Fire are along for the trek. For these freed slaves, the Three-in-One are up and running, bearing the pain of centuries and leading them home.

One of the things about which we humans chronically suffer amnesia is the revelation that God is always available to us, always tuned in to where we are and what we need. We become closed in, though. We're all like youth entranced by electronic screens and aware only of the music that wafts through earbuds. We narrow our world and tune out what is all around us. Yet God shouts "I AM!" through our inner din—and waits for us to look up, unplug, and listen.

Remove, O living God, the things that prevent me from noticing your nearness all the time and everywhere. Impress on me the understanding that you, as Spirit, hear cries and want to dry tears. Let me recognize that we stand together on holy ground.

≋ **FOR REFLECTION**

- Can I imagine what it must have been like to have that encounter with the burning bush on Mt. Horeb? If I had been in Moses' place, what do I think I would have felt?

- What does "I AM" (which mimics in syllables and accent one human heartbeat) mean to me as the name of God?

5 | A DIFFERENT SPIRIT

READ NUMBERS 14:5–25

> *But my servant Caleb, because he has a different spirit and has followed me wholeheartedly, I will bring into the land into which he went, and his descendants shall possess it.* NUMBERS 14:24

There are those who are wholehearted and those who are half-hearted. There are those who are faithful and those who fiddle, fudge, and compromise. One of God's disappointments with those who were liberated from slavery in Egypt was that they grew restive and self-absorbed, forgetful and stingy. They forgot who had liberated them, the God of their ancestors, and they grew fussy about food. They grew weary of the journey and turned to glitter and gloss.

We too can be tempted by golden calves.

So the question for us is how, amid a society that focuses on celebrity, comfort, and consumption, can we escape superficiality? How do we sustain a spirit that seeks depth, simplicity, and self-giving? Integrity and fidelity, unfortunately, tend to render a person out of step and downright odd. After all, appearances get attention, and undersides get gilded over. The rich and famous go on squandering the goods of the earth, ruining their marriages, soaking themselves in narcotizing pleasures, and stamping their names on things that get thrown away. The glitz is so appealing.

Meanwhile, the God of our ancestors in faith calls us to care for creation and love tenderly those to whom we have pledged our lives. We, like Caleb, are driven by that Spirit who differs from the spirit of the age. Without much ado, we are asked to stretch ourselves and keep stretching on account of others, on account of their good. We are to spend ourselves on projects that have lasting value.

Caleb, little known as he may be, is a man of virtue. He has scouted the Promised Land and returned to bring others along. He has never dreamed of cheapening himself. A grateful, humble spirit tends to remember that we are not our own and that our lives are not up for barter or pawn. If we sell out, that will only be because we have forgotten promises—ours to God and God's to us. We have decided that we'd rather be brokered off at a loss, for the sake of some transitory gewgaw or flimsy substitute for love.

≋ **PRAYER**

God, let me remember that you are the center of my life. Give me your Spirit, no matter how different or out of sync it may make me seem.

≋ **FOR REFLECTION**

- We have all met Calebs—the unheralded people who are faithful, trustworthy, and selfless. They are humbly dutiful and make sure that wheels turn and good things happen. Who have been the Calebs in my life? Who are the ones I count on for goodness and (to use a good old Christian word) righteousness?

- What do I consider some of the great religious or spiritual advances that have been made by nameless or lesser known people? Do I recall those people on All Saints Day?

6 | CLOSE AT HAND

READ DEUTERONOMY 30:11-20

Surely this commandment that I am commanding you today is not too hard for you, nor is it too far away. It is not in heaven...Neither is it beyond the sea...No, the word is very near to you; it is in your mouth and in your heart for you to observe. DEUTERONOMY 30:11–14

There is a New Age sense of a Me-god within and a contrasting Christian sense of God-with-us, a God who is also within us, the indwelling Trinity. New Age religion seems to say that we all are gods and can both summon and craft our own god. Christianity says that God, who is author of the universe and risen Son, breathes into us the Spirit of life, truth, beauty, love. The Holy Spirit is the wisdom we can tap and the true north on the compass of our lives. God's word is, in the end, quite simple. God's word, God's command, is that we live and love reverently. This means acknowledging the God who is both other and ours, honoring the life we have been given, regarding humanity as our family, and treating the created world with respect.

That is not too abstract to grasp. What is difficult for us is to apply the simple dictum of living in relationship. It is far too easy for us to serve up excuses for our lapses and hand off responsibility to others. Being law-abiding, in God's sense, is heeding the Spirit, who calls us to live with care and kindness. Being observant not just of commandments but of God's vital, real presence means that we look deep within. God's Spirit, God's command, is our best and most original intuition.

As Moses concludes his farewell address to Israel, he reminds the people that the command of God is, at heart, a call to "choose life so that you and your descendants may live." Choosing life means that we live gently and nurture life around us. It means that we exude spirit and strength. In the end, it means that we leave, in our wake, a quality of life that can, and wants to, live on.

Spirit of God, make me heedful of the word you speak simply in the sounds of each day. Make me one who supports, encourages, and enriches the life around me.

≋ **FOR REFLECTION**

- In what ways do I keep in touch with the God in my heart?

- If I were able to craft the future, what sort of world would I pass on to the generations coming after me?

- What small steps do I take each day to show reverence for human life, creaturely life, and the natural world?

7 | THE SPIRIT UPON DAVID

≋ **READ 1 SAMUEL 16:1-13**

Then Samuel took the horn of oil, and anointed him in the presence of his brothers; and the spirit of the Lord came mightily upon David from that day forward. 1 SAMUEL 16:13

The stories of the great King David are marvelous and retold three thousand years after he lived. His canny defeat of Goliath with a slingshot and five smooth stones, the military victories that followed, his fond friendship with Saul's son Jonathan, his skill at lyre and song, and his respectful treatment of a darkly depressed and insanely jealous King Saul are part of salvation history. So too are his reverence for the Ark of the Covenant, his desire to build a temple, and his lifelong composition of psalms. All of these are things for which we remember David. We also know of his fall from grace and his candid confession of guilt and genuine repentance.

One of David's many hymns demonstrates how God dwelt and dealt with him:

> The spirit of the Lord speaks through me, his word is upon
> my tongue. The God of Israel has spoken, the Rock of Israel
> has said to me: One who rules over people justly...is like the
> light of morning, like the sun rising on a cloudless morning,
> gleaming from the rain on grassy land.   2 SAMUEL 23:2-4

There was about David an aura of splendor, joy, and awe.

We tend to forget that he was the eighth son of Jesse to be considered when Samuel came to anoint someone to succeed Saul. As the youngest and the one out herding sheep, he was deemed the least likely. Later, despite the sincerity of his love for God, David suffered family tragedies and anguish over the royal succession. David, however, remained faithful, and though his power seemed expansive, he let himself be subject to prophet and priest. David had humble beginnings and ended humbly, uninflated by all his victories and accomplishments.

The Spirit upon David connects us with the humble beginnings of the Son of David, the Messiah, and the circumstances of his entry into the world. Bethlehem did not seem to be the likeliest city from which God's anointed would come. Perhaps Poland and, first Albania and then India, did not seem to be the most likely places from which two saints—a globally known pope and a Nobel Peace Prize winner—would come.

≋ PRAYER

Holy God, call to mind for me the fact that you tend to choose the unsuspecting, the unlikely, and out-of-the-way places when your anointed ones and your heroes emerge. Don't let me jump to conclusions about who should be chosen to spread your word and do your work. Appearances do not faze you. Give me the grace to see where Davidic hearts are, beyond the externals.

≋ FOR REFLECTION

- When we sing "O Little Town of Bethlehem," do I tend to glamorize it? Do I remember that it was a place of sheepherders and stables? Why do I suppose that God anoints people from such inconspicuous beginnings?

- Of the one hundred and fifty psalms, which two or three can I identify as my favorites? What is it about them that moves me?

8 | THE SPIRIT THAT CARRIED ELIJAH

≋ **READ 1 KINGS 18** AND **2 KINGS 2:1-15**

*"As soon as I have gone from you, the spirit of the Lord will carry you
I know not where; so, when I come and tell Ahab and he cannot find you,
he will kill me, although I your servant have revered the Lord from my
youth."* 1 KINGS 18:12

Over the years of his prophetic career, Elijah had servants, messengers
who came back and forth to find him, people who benefited from his
healing and his prayers, challengers in the persons of the priests of Baal,
monarchs who pursued him, and a successor, Elisha, who carried on
his work.

Ahab, husband of Jezebel, was, of course, one of the evil kings in
the line of David's descendants. The two together were a couple that
wrought havoc on Israel. Not surprisingly, Obadiah, sent to arrange a
meeting between Ahab and Elijah, feared for his life. The king and his
queen had murderous reputations. Elijah, Obadiah knew, had a knack
for evading slaughter and for periodically disappearing.

The story of Elijah's contest with the priests of Baal is a legendary
one. He taunts them, telling them their god must be meditating or mean-
dering or away on a trip or sleeping when they fail to summon fire for
their sacrifice. Then Elijah performs what must have seemed an extreme
magic trick, by calling down fire after he has doused kindling and the
stacked wood with water and then having his sacrifice consumed. It is
a demonstration of his God's might, his God's power over nature, his
God's command of every situation.

The exhausted Elijah disappears to Mount Carmel and is shortly on
the run. When we read the story, we know that there is more than one
way in which the spirit of the Lord carries him. Eventually he comes back
to prophesy again.

"Swing Low, Sweet Chariot" sings out the later story, the one recalled
symbolically at every Seder supper, where a place is set for Elijah. When

Elijah has clinched the agreement to pass his mantle to Elisha, "a chariot of fire and horses of fire" sweep down. Then Elijah disappears in a whirlwind. That explains why many centuries later Israelites were still waiting for Elijah to return and thought that the appearance of John the Baptist and Jesus of Nazareth opened the possibility that he might indeed have come back as one or the other.

We don't really know what this carrying off of Elijah means. We do know that his occasionally dispirited spirit always revived, and wonders never ceased. In his disappearance, we are reminded that God works in ways that confound us, in ways not bound by the norms of time and space.

Elijah himself was a wonder. Most wondrous of all was his courageous obedience to a nerve-wracking call.

⩥ PRAYER

God of deserts, fires, mountains, and skies, help me to know when to confront, how to act, where to speak, and how to rise up again after exhaustion, doubt, and fear. Help me recover when my limits are tested, and recall to me that you, in your Spirit, are the agent of my recovery.

⩥ FOR REFLECTION

- Elijah's story has miracles of healing, miracles of multiplication of food, and miracles over nature. He spent forty days and forty nights in the wilderness. He is said, by the gospels, to have appeared with Moses at the Transfiguration. Why does Elijah hold so significant a place among the prophets?

- How do we account for the fact that we have relatively little verbatim from Elijah, unlike the major and minor writing prophets? Does the lack of a Book of Elijah render him less effective?

- What lessons can I gain from the stories of Elijah having been "carried" by the Spirit?

9 | IN THE QUIET

📖 **READ 1 KINGS 19**

> *But the Lord was not in the wind; and after the wind an earthquake,*
> *but the Lord was not in the earthquake; and after the earthquake a fire,*
> *but the Lord was not in the fire; and after the fire a sound of sheer silence.*
>
> 1 KINGS 19:11B–12

In any life lived fully, in any life expended with vigor, there are likely to be times of burnout, disillusionment, exhaustion, and terror. The faithful mind recalls that God's Spirit continues to hover over all and continues to wrest progress and sense from calamity, but the nerve endings forget.

It is a very tired and very distraught Elijah who journeys on to the wilderness after a collapse under a broom tree and after being nourished with angel food. It is an Elijah who doubts that there will ever again be strength for anything, except perhaps to wait and see if this one promise, that God will pass by, will actually be kept.

Every one of us has times of exhaustion and downbeat. We've probably never had a wicked queen post a notice for us—Wanted, Dead or Alive—or set out on a plot with poisoned apples. For us, that's the stuff of a Western or a Disney feature cartoon.

Yet we do have occasions to fear for our lives. There are health crises, natural disasters, bizarre traffic accidents, attacks by suicide bombers, economic implosions, and vile slanders that can move in to unravel us. When we are beset by any of them, we stop in our tracks. We hesitate before God-knows-what.

Elijah knew his mission, better and more clearly than we do. He could name his enemy, too, without cloud and doubt. But we know that he continued to believe in the reality and power of God, without the ambivalence of twenty-first century sophisticates. Even so, he became fatigued beyond words, stressed beyond stress, and unstrung. For Elijah, the Spirit in the sheer silence did one thing: The Spirit restored his confidence. The Spirit repaired his shredded will so that he could go on.

For us, faith has to lure us sometimes, somewhere, to some still spot so that we can just wake up.

We need a good night's sleep. A non-arthritic stretch. A bounce of morning sun and breeze and dew to quicken our steps. A smile and an assurance that we matter. We need that when we're at our lowest and most lost. After catastrophe. After trauma.

Elijah listened to the silence, gathered up strength, reaffirmed his purpose, and set out, on divine command, for Damascus.

In the quiet of a dark place, we need to watch and wait and expect a strengthening question, a new goal. We need to listen for a voice issuing from sheer silence. If it truly comes unbidden and from beyond ourselves, we can be fairly certain that it is God's signal to get up and go.

⇛ PRAYER

Out of my collapse and from within my terror, let me hear your voice, Lord, in that silence. Then give me spirit to move on.

⇛ FOR REFLECTION

- Sister Mary Catherine Hilkert, OP (in Donnelly, 62-63) has remarked that Cardinal Suenens, a major figure in Vatican II and champion of the charismatic renewal, experienced for a time a "dark night of hope." He was troubled by lagging energy and dismal global events. Yet he carried on evangelical and ecclesiastical duties vigorously. He trusted the Spirit and asked, "Who would dare to say that the love and imagination of God were exhausted?" When have I had to rouse myself similarly?

- How do I pray when I feel empty inside? What natural, earthly things seem to perk me up and give me more spiritual vim? In other words, how do grace and nature work together for me?

10 | A DOUBLE PORTION OF THE SPIRIT

READ 2 KINGS 2

> *When they had crossed [the Jordan], Elijah said to Elisha, "Tell me what I may do for you, before I am taken from you. Elisha said, "Please let me inherit a double share of your spirit."* 2 KINGS 2:9

Elisha was a plowboy or a young plowman when Elijah conscripted him to be his servant. Apparently, some years had passed when Elijah and Elisha arrived in Bethel, and Elisha was greeted by local prophets with a question: "Do you know that today the Lord will take your master away?" Elisha somehow knows, and he is determined not to leave Elijah alone.

When Elijah is swept away, Elisha is the eyewitness, and this assures him that he has received the prophet's spirit twofold. He shortly learns that he can part water, purify a drinking supply, save a woman's children from sale into slavery, restore two dead sons, provide grain amidst a famine, and command the cleansing of Namaan. He anoints Jehu king of Israel to defeat Ahab and Jezebel and, initially, drive out the remnants of the worship of Baal. Unfortunately, Elisha's possession of the double portion of Elijah's spirit did not spare the people the effects of the free will of kings and captains of armies.

The seesaw of fidelity-infidelity, restoration of the Covenant-abandonment of it, continued down until the time of Christ.

There are many reasons—human fragility and honest perception of our own inadequacies among them—that cause us to feel that we need more and more and more talent, stick-to-it-iveness, and grace. There are also reasons why we are able to accomplish more than we might ever have imagined. When God's Spirit works within us, we exceed ourselves. We may surpass our mentors. But we cannot force people to act virtuously. We cannot coerce sanctity. No matter what displays of God's power we offer or what example of good character we show, people are not prevented from surrendering to their temptations—even their demons.

Elisha, like Elijah, found that. For all his trouble and his authentic proclamation of God and God's justice, he was still, somewhere inside, the plowboy who had to say goodbye to his parents and the bald-headed man taunted by little boys.

When he died, though, they found that he still had life-giving qualities. A dead man rose.

⇒ PRAYER

Spirit of truth and justice, help me to ask for what I need and to use what I receive.

⇒ FOR REFLECTION

- Mercy Amba Oduyoye, a Ghanaian theologian, has spoken of how proverbs and folktales can be revelatory sources for marginalized peoples. She speaks of "the charism of the voiceless," the cry of the poor (in Donnelly, 103–108, 113–121). How does Elisha seem to exemplify the ability of the poor to rise and, when the time is right, to find a powerful voice?

- Who are the formerly voiceless who are exercising their charisms in our time?

11 | WHAT HULDAH HAD TO SAY

≋ READ 2 CHRONICLES 34

*So Hilkiah and those whom the king had sent went to the prophet
Huldah, the wife of Shallum the son of Tokhath son of Hasrah, keeper
of the wardrobe...She declared to them, "Thus says the Lord, the God
of Israel..."* 2 CHRONICLES 34:22–23

A prophet is one who sees through to the depths of things, speaks the
truth of things, and often can foresee the consequences of choices that
have been made. Such was Huldah, from whom the king wished counsel
regarding what would happen to Israel and Judah in light of their history of violations of God's law, recently found in the neglected temple
in Jerusalem.

Josiah was one of the virtuous descendants of David. He devoted his
thirty-one-year reign to restoration of the temple and rededication of the
people to God's word and the Book of the Law. He did penance for the
offenses both Israel and Judah had committed against it. He was well dis-
posed to heed both warnings and promises.

Huldah's words cut to the quick, but Josiah recognized the justice
in them. Clearly it was the first time that many of them, craftsmen and
governors, had actually heard a recitation of the Torah. She, who knew
its heart, advised the king that Judah would be besieged because of the
laxity of God's chosen people. The king, who proceeded with a public
renewal of the covenant and a purging of all the remnants of idolatry,
made sure that Passover was kept and that the Law was held in reverence.
The people of Jerusalem and Benjamin recommitted themselves, and it
is said of Josiah that "all his days they did not turn away from following
the Lord the God of their ancestors."

Huldah also assured Josiah that the nobility of his heart and his very
real humility were known to God. Because of that, he would pass peace-
fully in death before the coming of any wrath.

This woman, rarely mentioned in the record of Old Testament heroism, stands out as one who saw clearly and knew the Law by having lived it. She was able to read the mind of God. The Spirit within her served to re-outfit her people in grace even as the king in sorrow was tearing his clothes.

⇒ PRAYER

Spirit of God, there are those whose testimony is utterly reliable. Help me to seek them out, especially when I need to understand you and your eternal Word.

⇒ FOR REFLECTION

- Huldah stands with such women as Deborah and Jael in the Book of Judges and then Ruth, Judith, and Esther. The king and the priest Hilkiah defer to her wisdom and judgment. St. Catherine of Siena, an advisor and chider of the pope, was among those of the Christian era of her ilk. Who are some of the women I have heard of or known who surpassed the understanding of those in power? How did they or have they drawn the powerful to work for the good?

12 | A NEW SONG, NEW SONGS

READ JUDITH 16:1–17

Let all your creatures serve you, for you spoke, and they were made.
You sent forth your spirit, and it formed them. JUDITH 16:14

Sometimes our efforts at getting worship music lively and relevant have silly results. One of the attempts at a contemporary version of the Jewish Hallel hymn, frequently used on Holy Thursday, sounds like a variation on the washtub song of Snow White's seven dwarfs. There are worse examples.

The impulse, however, is noble.

Judith, a heroine of Israel, desired to sing a new song, even though its lyrics took their prompt from what we know as Psalm 104. Mary, in response to Elizabeth's greeting, spoke her canticle in echoes of the one chanted by Hannah, mother of Samuel, a thousand years before. From Thomas Aquinas to the brothers of Taizé, and long before, believers have been sounding hymns to celebrate the living bread.

We do the same with songs about America and certainly with songs of love. We can never express enough admiration for a great land, and we can never say "I love you" too often, even if the melody, the harmony, the choruses, and the instruments keep changing.

Judith notes that the spirit of God fashioned creatures, and all of them somehow wished to mount their praise. She does this in a song of thanksgiving for her rescue of the people from a horrendous enemy. A contemplative at heart, and in her life prior to the entry into Holofernes' household, Judith acts in the service of the God of Israel and of her people. The turn to triumphant, grateful song comes to her inevitably as prayer.

Music itself is a kind of service, just as it so often is prayer. Instrumentals often lift our minds and hearts to God. Adagios and slow dances and smooth jazz tenderize our affections and calm our jangled nerves. Country music twangs us to the practical and down-to-earth.

Marches, pizzicatos, jive, rock, and hip-hop rouse us, up our pulses, get us hand-clappingly, foot-stompingly, even car-rumblingly excited. Masses and classical symphonies render us reverent.

Where there is rhythm there is life. And where there are makers of music there are always new ways to express ancient and universal things. Perhaps that's why, as young schoolchildren have said, certain songs "get stuck in your head."

Somehow, the Creator Spirit, spoken forth by the creating God, keeps inspiring song. And the songs, old and new, ingenious or trite, serve so many purposes.

⟫ PRAYER

God, I praise you in plain English and in ordinary words, but I also sing, in whatever languages I can, the words of your glory. Help me always appreciate the way in which your Spirit sets me on right paths and works good for our lives.

⟫ FOR REFLECTION

- Judith's high priests and the elders hailed her as "the glory of Jerusalem,…the great boast of Israel,…the great pride of our nation!" (Judith 15:9). Catholicism applies these laudatory words to the Blessed Mother. How would I compare and contrast the two?

- Mary had Gabriel. How do I imagine that Judith knew that God's Spirit was pressing her to shocking action?

- The end of her book says that Judith spent the rest of her life honored and famous but in preferred seclusion. How is it that those who do amazing things often wish to retire from the public eye? What do I suppose I would do if I were in such a situation?

13 | FAR AND AWAY

READ PSALM 33

By the word of the Lord the heavens were made, and all their host by the breath of his mouth. PSALM 33:6

It's more likely these days to get a sense of the wild array of lighted sky in a planetarium than it is in one's own backyard or at a beach. From the sky down, in jet-path, it is easier to see a refulgence of light below than it is to see light from the ground up. There's the moon, yes, and the Big and Little Dipper, and Orion, and sometimes the evening star, but hardly anyone sees more without a telescope. And only a few stay up in August for the Perseid meteor shower.

Whether or not we see, the hosts of the heavens are there. We can craft sky maps and sky domes and talk about the red planet and the rings of Saturn and black holes and wildly distant galaxies. We have that red shift evidence that has told the story of an expanding universe. What we don't yet know is whether the Big Bang is headed out to a strung-out Big Scatter or destined eventually to double back into a Big Crunch. One scenario is an exhaling that stretches out indefinitely. The other is an in-drawn suction that ends in a little puff of breath.

The truth is that no matter how much we know of astronomy and cosmology, we don't know much. Some scientists and philosophers posit that it all just happened—a sudden vacuum fluctuation, say, setting everything in motion. Out of nowhere. Beyond reason. Think Carl Sagan, Stephen Hawking, Stephen Weinberg, Richard Dawkins. Others say that the stupendousness of it all points back to a grand design, which implies a cosmic intelligence. Robert Jastrow, Paul Davies, Stanley Jaki, and, at moments, Einstein would be among these.

Those of us who buy into the Judaeo-Christian and Islamic traditions say God did it. Complexity and diversity and light, light, light started as breath. The Hebrew Bible calls it "a wind from God," calling order from chaos (Genesis 1:2). The Christian Scriptures speak of wisdom in the making of the world and the crafting of ourselves (Ephesians 1:8). The Koran identifies Allah, full of wisdom, as the one who sends winds at the origin of the world (Surah 37). For all of the Abrahamic religions, God creates in wisdom and currents of air. Then light comes.

Perhaps that is why not only wind and breath but light too are our catechetical symbols of the Spirit.

As Spirit-bearers, we too are called to shed light in dark places, to shine like full sky, and to guide like a beacon. It's important that we not be dimmed by all our artificial lights. Sometimes the Spirit asks us to stand against black night as just *us*. Unclouded and uncomplicated. Even though we don't know the whole of history or the details of the universe's destiny, we do know some key things we can share. Especially about the one who began the beginning.

⫸ PRAYER

Creator God, the word of your mouth gave forth light. Let whatever I say somehow be your shining speech, and let your Spirit breathe clear sky into and around me.

⫸ FOR REFLECTION

- When I reflect on the beginning of the universe and of us, how do I imagine it? Can I reconcile my faith with scientific accounts? Do I have the knowledge and tools needed to do so? If not, where might I find help?

- Somehow the breath of the Spirit blows darkness open into light. Can I find any comparisons in the natural world or even in my home as to how that might happen?

14 | THE MISERERE

READ PSALM 51:1–17

Have mercy on me, O God, according to your steadfast love…Create in me a clean heart, O God, and put a new and right spirit within me.

PSALM 51:1, 10

Psalm 51 is the Friday morning psalm, a penitential psalm. It's a psalm that reminds us that we have things to be sorry for. It also reminds us that God is merciful and full of "steadfast love," a recurrent phrase in Scripture. This psalm asks for something new, squeaky clean, and righteous in us. While we remain in many ways the same old selves, we keep seeking renewal of heart and soul. And we are confident that God can do it.

As we recite Psalm 51, we are not supposed to be morose, but we are supposed to be realistic. We admit that we have done wrong and that we have been born into a world in which a lot of evil goes on. We know that we have been caught up in evildoing and that we need to hang our heads in shame. But we also know that God continues to care for us and that there is a "joy of [God's] salvation" always available to us. God doesn't care about burnt offerings but is gladdened by a couple of things: prayerful praise and a "broken and contrite heart."

That does not mean that God wants sackcloth and ashes or that God is happy to see us drooping around looking miserable. What it does mean is that God wants our honesty and genuine remorse.

We need moments of soul searching. We have not lived unsullied lives, and we have not gotten away without leaving a trail of tears somewhere. So we ought to have regrets. When we ask to be justified it isn't a bid for easy excuses. It's a request to be set right again with God and others. What that takes is laying our situation out frankly and counting on the extravagance of God's steadfast love. We ourselves have broken spirits, and we have done some breaking of hearts. Mercy!

Do, Lord, have mercy. Help me to use our penitential seasons and our penance services well. Turn my heart back and steady my stumbling. Heal those I have hurt. Spill your mystical grace on them. Clean up anything in me that still does harm.

⫸ **FOR REFLECTION**

- Why have St. Faustina and the Divine Mercy devotions become so popular? Why do I suppose St. John Paul went so far as to declare the Sunday after Easter Divine Mercy Sunday?

- Why, in an age that is so hep on positive self-image, does Holy Mother Church find it healthy to remind us that we are capable of doing wrong and that we do indeed do it?

15 | ASPIRATIONS

🔊 **READ PSALM 55**

And I say, "O that I had wings like a dove! I would fly away and be at rest." PSALM 55:6

Negi was what they called her, short for Negrita, the little black girl. Esmeralda Santiago, later a Harvard graduate, tells of a childhood riddled with stench, termites, corrugated metal walls, mud floors, and rivulets along pebbled streets that were the spillways of primitive latrines. In her barrio, *papis* worked from early morning dark to evening dark, and some drank hard, and visited whores, and *mamis* suffered the care of seven or eleven children who spent as much time outside as possible.

Perhaps it comes as a surprise to readers of *When I Was Puerto Rican* to find that Negi could celebrate the smells and tastes of the open markets and the hovels filled with the aromas of home cooking. She learned to catalog the flowers, the trees, and the birds. She relished her school uniforms and the virtual arcade of games the children made up.

Her father led rosaries and novenas when someone in the barrio died, but the family never had the children baptized, never went to Mass, and never prayed. She learned a bit about Father, Son, and Holy Spirit on brief visits to her *abuela*, her grandma, and she remarked on the dynamics of stand, bless, sit, stand, cross, sit, stand, kneel, line up, kneel, stand again at Mass. Her *abuela*, like so many for so many generations, kept holy water at the doorway of her house.

Though Negi grew to rebel and critique the violence and degrading conditions of the slums of her youth, she also came to more. What some would shuck off as childish daydreams she turned into more mature goals. She was fired by literature, drama, dance, and song. Somehow the rich floral designs of her mother's dresses and the pennants and signs of her old city had put color and music and flounce into her.

Esmeralda's inspirations fueled her aspirations all the way to New York's High School of Performing Arts and Harvard and then to a successful career as a writer and entrepreneur. It's not a mistake that inspiration and aspiration have the word "spirit" as their root.

We religious people tend to gussy up inspiration. We think the Spirit is embodied in our cadences and blessings and candles and vestments. Embodied the Spirit may be, but not confined. The Spirit lends dove wings wherever hearts lift with hope for better things.

The psalmist knew that the Spirit tells forth from creation, even in meager Mideast deserts and thinning fields. Even in barrios with sewers for streets and hurricanes heaving plywood and cooking pots beyond the borders of barrios. Even in Brooklyn neighborhoods with graffiti on walls, creaking stairs, and people lounging on stoops.

The Spirit is quite capable of shining forth from star-studded skies and also slithering down slimy streets and subway tunnels. Negi may not have named her drives and ambitions religious or spiritual, but the engineer of her breakout would certainly seem the same one who rides "on the wings of the wind" and renews individual lives as well as the whole earth.

⇒ PRAYER

Lord, lift me up from wherever I've found degradation. Hold out to me the hope for more. And give me spirit, smiles, and lifelong aspirations.

⇒ FOR REFLECTION

- What memoirs or stories have inspired me and given me models of growing up and breaking free?

- Who are my heroes and who are the persons who have lent me dove wings?

- Is it possible to be both humble and high-achieving? How does that work?

16 | RENEWING THE EARTH

🔖 **READ PSALM 104**

When you send forth your spirit, they are created; and you renew the face of the ground. PSALM 104:30

Every now and then there comes a moment when we feel our lives are truly magical. In spite of everything that dismays and dislodges us, we catch a glimpse of cardinals flitting through stripped winter trees or spot a streetlight's glow on the back of a clay-colored frog out for a night of early summer leaping.

It may be a dank night in a southern clime, draped in Spanish moss and fanned by fern and palm. It may be an autumn day up north when yellow, russet, and purple mums dot bright gardens and corn husks turn tallow-colored and lank amid pumpkin time. In that southern place, tweeting continues on, and azaleas bloom month after month. In the north, the fields grow freckled with brown leaves, sun splashes on ponds and silos and church steeples, as gun barrels glint, borne by orange hunters spotting small game.

Back along Goose Woods Trail, some Pennsylvanian strollers sight the claw marks of raccoons in fresh mud. Wood pewees and gray catbirds flit and mock and mew back in the bush. Cardinals and scarlet tanagers light from branch to branch, and woodpeckers, dizzy as ever, hang upside down on a bucking branch, their black and red-orange splotched heads bobbing below freckled white bellies. The wind blows, and a wooden bridge over a thin creek lightly rocks. Noonday stands, and color, movement, sound, and light all gad breezily about. Beneath the clods and rocks, something new begins a beat, a scrabble for life, a poking about.

Meanwhile, down at the marsh edge down Mattis Road on St. Helena Island in South Carolina, the tide goes down, and an alligator snout appears. An egret flaps for a small fish, then heads into a clump of trees. The shrimp boats heave out, and in Port Royal Sound the dolphins leap. The lapping waves dazzle with liquid diamonds as they bob and play.

There are reasons why mortal creatures sometimes seem to have permanent smiles on their faces.

⪩ PRAYER

I exult, yes, and glorify you, God, for everything lovely and new. Help me remember always to be thankful and to know that the diverse creatures all around are blessing upon blessing.

⪩ FOR REFLECTION

- Beauty itself is understood by saints and theologians to be a sign and gift of God. What natural beauty surrounds me? How often do I notice?

- What human-made beauty is inspired by the beauty of nature? Can I say that I have contributed to that beauty—by, say, presenting food beautifully, planting a garden, crafting furniture or metal work, painting and repairing?

- If I have lived more than one place in my lifetime, where would I say I have felt closest to the Spirit and the Spirit's work of renewing the earth?

17 | NOWHERE TO HIDE

➤ **READ PSALM 139:1–18**

Where can I go from your spirit? Or where can I flee from your presence?
PSALM 139:7

You can head out of Grand Marais in the upper peninsula of Michigan and point west for a stop at Dog Patch, a bar and restaurant in Munising, with the idea of getting eventually to Marquette. The maps show a secondary road that looks like a fairly direct way to Route 2. The surprise is that some miles into the trip it turns into a bumpy sand and gravel lane through wild expanses of trillium and tall pines. The only humans along the way are bearded, flannel-shirted, unshaven guys in pickup trucks with gun racks.

You realize that if you ever needed a hideout, this would be the place to pitch a camouflage tent and spread branches and fallen leaves over your car.

Somehow, though, you know that you would not be able to run away from yourself. Your hopes and dreams, your griefs and diseases, your blessed memories and your weighty sins would all be there. You might fancy that it is possible to reinvent yourself and take on a new identity, but the you-ness of you would remain. There is a spirit within that always wants to be outed. It bubbles up from time to time even in the amnesiac or the senile. It's the stowaway who is always along for the ride.

Similarly, we find that the imposing reality of God can never quite be avoided. Something is always there that suggests a life force and life source, a deep goodness, that is behind it all. And that being tends to haunt us and taunt us, even if only in a quick glimpse of a V-formation of Canada geese or a rookery of blue herons high in the crowded trees. God is there in the dunes and the clefts of Pictured Rocks just beyond Au Sable. The waggle of the fox beating it down the road and the startled look of the family that thought this was a tight little highway too—these somehow flash God signs.

The problem is that God, that inescapable Supreme Being, always wants to get a word in edgewise. And we find that God's spirit keeps wafting around us, even when we fancy ourselves in the middle of nowhere and in the best of hideouts. There is a pulse in the silence that isn't just ours.

⪦ PRAYER

Dear Lord, if I had listened to your psalmist David, I would have known that there is no fleeing you. Your spirit seeps up even from the squish of rut-mud and moss.

⪦ FOR REFLECTION

- The biblical Book of Jonah is one famous narrative of a runaway. *Les Miserables*, whether Hugo's novel or the musical, tells a fugitive story too. How is it that those on the run don't tend to fare very well, even if they manage to do some good while they are running?

- When have I found that I took myself with me when I was trying to escape something?

- Do I truly have confidence that God's Holy Spirit knows me through and through and loves me with my mix of good and bad, certainty and confusion? When does that confidence hit me?

18 | MEMORY

➔ **READ PROVERBS 3:1–26**

*Long life is in [Wisdom's] right hand; in her left hand are riches
and honor…She is a tree of life to those who lay hold of her.*

PROVERBS 3:16, 18

In a matter of months, a man who has managed sales and overseen a
maintenance crew can sink into an old settee and consume his days with
John Wayne reruns and ball games, at the end of which he never can
recall the scores. Then in a few more months he forgets names, confuses
2 AM with rising time, and wanders. Then he cannot figure what to do
with a hammer and nail or a wrench or a screwdriver. Finally, he stares
at the spoon in his cereal bowl and sits motionless till someone comes
to feed him.

One of life's miseries is the onslaught of dementia and the ravages
of Alzheimer's. Disease itself—chronic illness, critical illness, mental illness—and the array of types of disability are ongoing enigmas. We may
find some measure of correction, assistance, and even cure, but we still
are puzzled to our depths with the question of why things go so wrong
and some conditions are incurable.

Original sin is the easy dogmatic answer. Built into the structure of
our world is some way-back disharmony. There is, in our race at least, an
inborn tendency to want to be sovereign over everything and to resist
order and discipline, even when these are good for us. That's a given.
Those who have no religious bent have days when they can identify
with Jeremiah's exasperated lament: "Cursed be the day on which I was
born!" (Jeremiah 20:14). We sometimes find ourselves fleeing for cover
and wishing life itself would run a shorter course.

Our souls are racked when we face innocent suffering. It's somehow
easier to confront the problem of evil when we can identify a perpetra-
tor—a crazed dictator, a serial killer, a drunk repeat offender—and pin
crimes on him or her. It's far worse when we face the death of a child—

or the decline of a formerly very high-functioning elder who now needs hand-holding and a bib.

We cannot figure what the God's-eye view of all this could possibly be.

Every now and then, though, we recall that there is Spirit as long as there is breath. The dying, speechless, bedfast sister begins to sing an old Latin hymn. The man who has lost all aptitudes stirs to greet a giggling toddler who springs into his arms. The child who has spent more time at St. Jude's than at home rouses gleefully at the sight of her real dog and her corral of rocking horses and stuffed animals. The family of a high school senior killed at an unmarked railroad crossing—when the bells didn't sound through her car's cranked-up music—funds a scholarship that will memorialize her for decades.

As long as we love, the Spirit indwells. As long as there are those who have known us live, our spirit dwells somehow in them.

That doesn't answer the larger questions, but it does point to a reality beyond our comprehension. There is a spirit world that eye does not see, and it suggests that somehow the fact of mere living matters. We may not get the sense of it. But life is somehow marked by Wisdom and is in her hands. Whether it is short or long. When it lingers. When we don't understand.

And life and we ourselves wisely go on.

⇛ **PRAYER**

God, I know that if I am wise, I am and will be a servant of life. Help me always to honor human life and treat persons with dignity no matter what their age or condition.

⇛ **FOR REFLECTION**

- What measures am I taking to try to help those long-living persons who are no longer the selves we once knew?

- What memories—personal, familial, or religious—do I play back over and over? Do I discipline myself to treasure positive memories of those I've loved and lost?

19 | DELIGHT

▶ READ PROVERBS 8

And I was daily God's delight, rejoicing before him always, rejoicing in his inhabited world and delighting in the human race. PROVERBS 8:30–31

In the insight of Solomon, Wisdom is an attribute, a virtue, a life-goal, and also a personal companion. She is an initiator and instigator who loves variety, color, growth, and motion.

She swathes a universe with galaxies and indigo wonder. She flashes light and warmth that awaken quartz, feather flare, morning glory, sunflower head, wheat field, ocean sparkle, lightning streak, and aurora in wild sky. She plays in the dirt, and soon furry bear cubs paw by, along with woolly sheep and woolly mammoths, sleek gazelles, stallions, and border collies rippling as they run.

She crafts and tinkers and laughs.

The mountain lions rumble and whippoorwills whoop, and scallop shells are purposeful. Wisdom reveres them, shaping all for reasons that exceed human use or ken. She gives them habitat, just as she gives us enclosure, family, and friends. She desires for us, as for them, glistening, open space for artistry and romp.

The virtue to which the conscious are called is recognition—recognition that all creation *is* for its own sake, for our sake, for the sake of the planet and the solar system and universe, and certainly for God's sake. It won't abide our disfiguring, desiccating, or driving away.

She won't either.

For she desires to cast life like a magic spell and a spill of stardust over all the earth in many and mysterious ways. She is, as several translations have it, a predecessor of earth, a presence, a kind of "master worker" or "craftsman," a youth ever at play. Wisdom calls herself "the forerunner of God's prodigies."

As she flings creation endlessly into kaleidoscopic patterns and as she multiplies delight, she serves one warning. If we ignore her, we do so at our own peril. Un-wisdom, anti-wisdom, has no sense of wonder, no reverence for God's goods, inflicts harm, and, in fact, loves death. Wisdom cautions us not to waste.

≡ PRAYER

God, I can imagine Wisdom as a young, clever, and wholesome adolescent girl flinging life like daisy petals and siftings of baby's breath all over the place. Help me to perceive playfulness in the world around me. And help me to treat the products of that play very well.

≡ FOR REFLECTION

- St. Thomas Aquinas has spoken of diversity and multiplicity as part of God's plan in and for creation. What creatures particularly evoke wonder and delight in me?

- How, concretely, do I help my own ecosystem to flourish?

20 | VAINGLORY

≣ **READ ECCLESIASTES 1**

> *I said to myself, "I have acquired great wisdom, surpassing all who were over Jerusalem before me..." And I applied my mind to know wisdom and to know madness and folly. I perceived that this also is but a chasing after wind.* ECCLESIASTES 1:16–17

Some academic types just think that if folks read a lot, or take more courses, or accumulate a wall full of diplomas, they will grow in wisdom.

Granted, there is a great and very fine commitment to learning in our inherited Jewish tradition. And part of the genius of St. Dominic's Order of Preachers is the pledge of its members to be immersed in life-long study.

But an accumulation of words and tomes may simply result in the accumulator's retention of what one university geography professor has termed "U.B.I.s"—useless bits of information. He thought it was helpful if students knew something about rock strata, moraines, wadis, meanders, and sinkholes. But he also realized that not everything in his collected lectures would matter much in terms of the well-being of generations to come. A sinkhole drops the altogether unsuspecting, and it helps people very little if someone nearby knows what to call the phenomenon as it sucks in homes and playing children.

That is not to belittle information and education. It is simply to acknowledge their limits, as Koheleth, the speaker here, is doing. Intensive study and breadth of learning can equip us to understand the world better and to help others interpret it. It may even assist them and us to live wisely and avail ourselves of the planet's resources and cultural riches more prudently. It may offer us lessons from history which will help us avoid war and negotiate peace.

But we have to admit that acquiring knowledge for its own sake, and knowledge of the most arcane matters, can be as mindless an undertaking as stacking beer cans neatly on a garage wall or collecting hundreds of T-shirts and baseball caps. They may prove that we have identified with a team, been somewhere, and done considerable drinking, but they provide little by way of lessons. Similarly, ingesting hallucinogens to see how they work may offer us an extreme experience, but that experience will not feed a hungry world.

The point Koheleth makes is that the pursuit of wisdom is beneficent and godly. It is designed to make us better people. The knowledge that we acquire is meaningful if it helps us to be more well-rounded and productive citizens and more humble saints. If it is merely decorative and frivolous, our learning has missed its proper destination.

⟫ PRAYER

Spirit of God, help me know what is good to know. Lead me to learn things that fill me with wonder at your works. Give me helpful clues about the mysteries of life and holiness. I want to spend the time I have profitably.

⟫ FOR REFLECTION

- When it comes to academics, what are my preferred areas of study? In what way are these things useful to me?

- Some courses and even whole departments get jettisoned when they don't seem to be profitable. Often the fine arts, philosophy, and theology get written off as impractical. What arguments can I make in favor of studying creative works and texts that delve into the deeper questions of life?

21 | BEFORE

⇒ **READ ECCLESIASTES 11:1—12:9**

> *Remember your creator in the days of your youth, before the days of*
> *trouble come,...before the silver cord is snapped, and the golden bowl*
> *is broken...and the dust returns to the earth as it was, and the breath*
> *returns to God who gave it.* ECCLESIASTES 12:1, 6, 7

Ecclesiastes is a perfect mid-life crisis book. It could be offered as a case study for what Erik Erikson termed the alternative to old age's achievement of integrity: despair, or nearly so.

All the things we have worked for and wanted aren't enough, we find. Nothing lasts. People die and projects go poof. Pleasures fade, and our blood pressure percolates. Energy goes plop, and enthusiasm fizzles down to flat.

Fortunately, the whole of Ecclesiastes doesn't read quite that way. There is the elegant hymnody at the beginning of chapter 3: the rhythmic recounting of the seasons for everything. There's also the admonition to cast one's bread on the waters, a gesture of preparedness and expectation of return. The hearer is encouraged to enjoy life while remembering too that only God is the know-it-all.

The remembrance of mortality has a power about it. While silver and gold go and dust simply dusts, we're enjoined to recall that there is a larger story and a world beyond, a world above, the spirit world. Koheleth, the convoker of an assembly, nudges us to recall that everything given goes back to the giver, God—in a breath.

If there's an underlying motif in Ecclesiastes, it's a call to have passion. Not a passion for that passel of passing things (all those vanities) but, rather, a passion for the Lord and Giver of Life who is as endless as air.

≋ **PRAYER**

Spirit who gives life with breath and raises it from dust, lead me away from vain pursuits and let me move with the rhythms of seasons into hours well spent. And protect me from chronic disillusionment.

≋ **FOR REFLECTION**

- There are people who would have a right to be full of self-pity. Paul Kalanithi, neurosurgeon, non-smoker, and author of *When Breath Becomes Air*, could easily have given in to resentment about his early onset of lung cancer. How do people like Kalanithi help me lift myself or let myself be lifted when I feel that life has been unfair?

- How do I take responsibility for being both optimistic and realistic, joyful and honest, daring and cautious? What helps me keep life in balance?

- Sometimes when people are downhearted, we are called literally to pray over them as well as for them. When have I seen the Spirit work when someone has laid hands in prayer over a person who has been suffering?

22 | SPEECH MATTERS

READ WISDOM 1:6–11

Because the spirit of the Lord has filled the world, and that which holds all things together knows what is said, therefore those who utter unrighteous things will not escape notice, and justice, when it punishes, will not pass them by. WISDOM 1:7–8

We've all heard the ditty about sticks and stones. The trouble is that it isn't true. Name-calling and word-slaps hurt. Sometimes they do long-term damage.

Everyone knows that gossip is a sin. Slander can summon a lawsuit. But that less heralded vice, detraction, gets less attention. It's the unnecessary telling of a negative truth, one that reflects badly on someone, which the hearer has no need or right to know. The woman at the end of the block has no role to play if someone's daughter has shoplifted. The guy plunked down on a spring-popping old sofa in his garage requires no information about another guy's gambling debts. But we go on tale-bearing.

Why? It just seems that we think news is at a premium and we collect virtual blue ribbons if we're the first to know and the first to tell.

Sometimes we happen on or overhear information that is colorful, startling, and troubling. Our Christian response should be to pray. If we invite others to pray, we should do so without spilling the particulars.

For good reason, the Book of Wisdom says that the repetition of unrighteous things and the telling of lies are punishable acts. People have been sent to prison and executed because of false witnesses. Perjurers have implicated others to save their own skins. Scandal-mongers have ruined the good names of honest and well-intended politicians and clergy, poisoned neighborhoods, alienated friends, and militated family members against one another. Whisperers have undermined morale in factories, offices, health care facilities, and schools by fueling doubts, suspicions, and fears.

The Spirit who has more than a bird's-eye view of the world and the gift of omniscience knows all this. Sometimes, unfortunately, there is hell to pay for the fires we've kindled and stoked.

≋ **PRAYER**

Spirit of truth and protector of justice, help me to remember that one of the goods held by persons is their reputation. Let me not be one who sullies it by misuse of that instrument, the tongue.

≋ **FOR REFLECTION**

- Scripture gives several powerful examples of those who were betrayed by others and suffered because of false accusations: Joseph, the son of Jacob and Rachel; Susanna; and, of course, Jesus. Can I name any occasions or situations in which I saw someone nearly ruined by rumors or by falsehood?

- "Wisdom is a kindly spirit," this book says. How can I resolve conflicts kindly?

23 | SOPHIA AND HER LURE

🎵 **READ WISDOM 7:1—8:20**

God loves nothing so much as the person who lives with wisdom. She is more beautiful than the sun, and excels every constellation of the stars.
WISDOM 7:28–29

In the wisdom literature of the Old Testament, the person or personification of Wisdom, is always She. *Hokmah* in Hebrew, *Sophia* in Greek: both are feminine. Wisdom is alluring, chaste, intelligent, strong.

Solomon recounts that there is a magnetic attraction to wisdom. John Shea, in a foreword written for Gregory Pierce's book on the theme, speaks of "the lure of the Kingdom of God" (Shea, in Pierce, *The World as It Should Be*, Loyola, 2010, x). Wisdom in all her glory draws us to herself. The biblical authors, particularly Solomon, Wisdom's champion, understood that drawing toward and drawing in as the tug of God.

Solomon acknowledges that he is "mortal, like anyone else," born "to breathe the common air," destined, like everyone, for "one entrance into life, and one way out." So he prays for more, for the abundance of wisdom, and God gives her. He finds wisdom to be both "unfailing treasure" and "friendship with God."

So Holy Wisdom is the desire of his heart, the pursuit of his life, and his bride. She is Solomon's teacher, and through her he learns astronomy, geography, botany, zoology, psychology, philosophy, virtue, jurisprudence, governance, and military strategy.

In religious education, as mentioned earlier, we speak of the importance of the *abuela*, the grandma, in inspiring prayerfulness in children. In matrimony, we talk of how manhood and womanhood grow and mature in the genuine friendship and mutual tenderness of husband and wife. In holy orders, we find so many deacons and priests who claim a mother, a female mentor, a religious sister, a favorite woman saint, and the Blessed Mother as the inspiration and encouragement of their vocations.

Every explorer needs a Sacagawea.

Every God-seeker and God-lover needs one who knows the topography of the Spirit. Solomon enumerates the stellar qualities of Sophia. She is possessed of a spirit that is "intelligent, holy, unique, manifold, subtle, mobile, clear, unpolluted, distinct, invulnerable, loving the good, keen, irresistible, beneficent, humane, steadfast, sure" and so much more. He names her the "fashioner of all things," the one who "pervades and penetrates all things," and "a breath and the power of God."

In other words, Wisdom is interior designer and design. She is the one who showcases all of creation and knows it inside out. She reads the mind of God and teaches the wise to read the book of life.

Wisdom is the eternal feminine: lover, birther, nurturer, teacher, guide, comforter, dazzling light, victor.

"Because of her," says Solomon, "I shall have immortality, and leave an everlasting remembrance to those who come after me."

⩵ PRAYER

You, Spirit, are a mesh of femininity and masculinity. Let me understand that your genderless self, your God-self, still carries the qualities I most admire in the great women who have touched my life. Help me to both appreciate and to emulate them.

⩵ FOR REFLECTION

- Wisdom is highlighted in the story of the women who both claim to be the mother of a living baby and point to the other as the mother of one who has died. When I recall Solomon's way of handling the dispute (1 Kings 3:16–28), how do I assess the risk he took in terms of the Spirit's gift of wisdom and the virtue of prudence?

- The Queen of Sheba was among the notables who heard of Solomon's wisdom and came to see for herself. She arrived from Ethiopia bearing a treasure trove of gifts. What am I willing to spend in terms of time and material resources to gain wisdom?

24 | SOLOMON'S PRAYER

➥ READ WISDOM 9

Send her forth from the holy heavens, and from the throne of your glory send her, that she may labor at my side, and that I may learn what is pleasing to you. WISDOM 9:10

One of life's challenges is figuring out how to gain and retain knowledge we ought to have and how to jettison what is useless and counter-productive.

Sometimes the task is quite straightforward. We need certain insights and cumulative information and skills to pay taxes, run a household, get diplomas, pass boards, and operate businesses or political campaigns or charitable institutions. We clearly don't need the headlines or interior content of the tabloids we see in the grocery line or the content of most ads, commercials, and pop-ups.

There are areas of learning that may be fruitful to us over the long term, and that is why we read, study, explore, go to conferences, and make retreats. Other things are downright harmful: prejudicial rantings, perjured testimony, false claims, pornography.

When we assay the barrage of information that comes at us, all of the above is obvious. What we can't always weigh or prioritize is what we most need. Solomon offers his guidance here.

We know well the account of God's proposal to give Solomon his heart's desire and his subsequent request for what is sometimes termed "an understanding heart," a.k.a. wisdom.

The Book of Wisdom recounts Solomon's prayer, a prayer raised even after he had studied widely and much. Somehow we all know that people can be very smart but not savvy in any practical way. They can be stuffed with gigabytes of data but lack common sense. They can be exceedingly learned but incompetent.

Solomon knew that he needed stellar guidance, holy insight, and lights larger and brighter than his own.

Thus, he had the savvy, the common sense, and the competence to pray for that spirit of God, God's wisdom, for all the leading anyone would need. Call it a grace.

≡ PRAYER

Good God, help me to exercise true wisdom in my choices, my diversions, my inquiries, and my use of time. Make me grow toward you. Give me both an understanding heart and a clear-thinking mind.

≡ FOR REFLECTION

- As I read Wisdom 9, what do I notice about Solomon's understanding of Wisdom? How do I relate it to my ongoing spiritual formation?

- If I were to make a list of books, retreats, parish missions, pilgrimages, or trips that have been sources of wisdom, what would I put on the list? What experiences at home or at work have also made me wiser? What might be some founts of wisdom I still need to explore?

25 | THE ISAIAH SCROLL

⇛ **READ ISAIAH 61:1–4** AND **LUKE 4:16–30**

The spirit of the Lord God is upon me, because the Lord has anointed me; he has sent me to bring good news to the oppressed, to bind up the brokenhearted, to proclaim liberty to the captives and release to prisoners; to proclaim the year of the Lord's favor... ISAIAH 61:1–2

When we read the major prophets, and when we read the Gospel according to St. Luke, we are always sure to hear this as the call to action on behalf of the lowliest of the lowly. We also are reminded of what must have been a stunning scene in Jesus' hometown synagogue.

This is the scroll, familiar to Jesus, which he asks for and reads one day in Nazareth. Then he takes a seat, ready to offer a commentary, and declares that this applies to him. He is anointed, he says. And the hearers are nonplussed. Then they begin to sneer and jeer.

We who have the post-resurrection, post-Pentecost perspective know, of course, that Jesus was right on the mark. This is exactly the mission he undertakes as Messiah: proclaiming glad tidings, making the broken whole, setting the locked-up and locked-in free, and showering good will and grace throughout the land. He seeks out the unremarkable and tends to souls' deepest needs. Applying this message from Isaiah to ourselves, though, seems more daunting than ascribing it to the Messiah of the world.

There are three very different ways in which we may go about applying it, ways that need to be questioned and probed.

The first may begin in a more grandiose way and then have to be toned down a bit. We acknowledge that we are disciples. We're baptized, confirmed churchgoers sent on mission. So, we listen to the call of the prophet and envision ourselves joining the Jesuit volunteers, feeding a few hundred at a soup kitchen, catechizing vagrants on streetcorners, hosting a drop-in center, being part of a Cursillo team, coordinating a pilgrimage of mercy to the state penitentiary, demonstrating at the capital against abortion or capital punishment. The grandiose scale is, however, hard to sustain. The buzz word *burnout* may set in rapidly. So maybe we are called to help the poor on another scale.

In this second case, it seems that the lowly one, the brokenhearted, the captive, the prisoner is one human being. It may be a family member with a serious disability or an elder in sudden decline. It may be a colleague or a close friend who seems to need more than the typical nurturing and support because of a devastating divorce, the revelation of a child's drug problem, a foreclosure, or an out-of-nowhere job loss. It may be that the Lord has anointed us to tend to this one, this certain special person, who becomes our child, our love, our companion, or our friend. It may be that the setting-free will happen only if we are the instruments.

The third way in which we may be invited to apply this scroll is related to the other two, but it turns them around—somewhat unexpectedly and even uncomfortably. We may find that we are the needy one, the one impelled to expose ourselves to being helped, to loosen up enough to be the recipient. It may be that we're the lowly, brokenhearted, captured, imprisoned one. We stand in need of a day or a year of jubilee. We are overdue for healing, and we will profit from respite and grace. We may recoil from the thought that we may have to surrender control, that we may not be the one dispensing charity to some poor other, that we may be the one who is, for the time, helpless. We would prefer that Christ's tending of us would be spiritual, not hard core, actual earthbound tending delivered to us by another or other human beings. It's easier to fancy ourselves the smiling benefactor of a cast of thousands than to see ourselves committed to the hidden life of another person. It's harder still to imagine that we are the beloved one in need of someone else's tending.

Sometimes we would prefer that the Lord sit down and just be quiet rather than start unrolling the scroll of ourselves. And we would be quite thrilled to have the Spirit invoked in such a way that we're the heroes rather than the ones all hollowed out.

HOLY WIND, HOLY FIRE

But sometimes the only way we can help is by having been helped. There's a huge spiritual leap in self-emptying. One way or another.

⇒ PRAYER

Lord, whether I am giver or receiver, let me know your anointing, and help me see the larger picture of your plan in and through the suffering of the world.

⇒ FOR REFLECTION

- Holy people through the centuries have offered their sufferings up. Father James Empereur, SJ, has said that for some the sacrament of anointing of the sick is a sacrament of vocation. Am I open to the possibility that some souls may be anointed to suffer on behalf of others?

- Overall, the Christian call is to relieve pain and to administer healing. That applies not only to others but to ourselves. We are meant to be healthy and whole. How do I balance care for others with my duty to care for my own health and well-being? How do I know when one or the other has gone overboard?

26 | A NEW COVENANT

⇒ READ JEREMIAH 31:15-17, 23-34

This is the covenant that I will make with the house of Israel after those days, says the Lord: I will put my law within them, and I will write it on their hearts; and I will be their God, and they shall be my people.

JEREMIAH 31:33

After dark comes morning light. After furious storms comes the sun. After battle comes truce. That is what we sigh for, and our sighs are soulful. Sometimes all we long for is unspeakable, inaudible. We are so weary of affliction or wrongdoing or violence that we are dumbed.

Jeremiah speaks of Rachel weeping for her children. Her scene, the scene of a victim's mother, has been repeated over and over throughout human history. The Holocaust of World War II, the Bosnian-Serbian conflict, the ceaseless uproars in the Middle East, the Hutu massacres of Tutsis in Rwanda, the plight of the Syrian refugees, the victims of suicide bombers: the list goes on and on and on. And in our own streets we suffer police versus slum dweller, gang turf wars, racial profiling, white versus black, Anglo versus Chicano, men versus women, molesters versus children, homegrown terrorists and haters of Muslims squaring off. All that comes of it is bloodshed and more hate. Life costs us tears.

What Jeremiah foresees is an end to all this. He forecasts possibility. And the possibility is both concretized and spiritualized. Concretely, he expects God, whose love is everlasting, to raise the chosen people back to a condition of self-sufficiency and even prosperity. He anticipates a kind of restoration of theocracy, a government that rules by God's law, by Torah. He projects a covenant that is known innately and engraved by the Spirit on the heart. He hopes a universal instinct for good will reign.

Christians see the fulfillment of this new covenant in Christ. They know, though, that covenant binding and covenant keeping are not simply matters of sealing parchment with a king's signet or, in more current terms, getting a notary public to stamp and date. They are matters of the heart.

And, unfortunately, a covenant cannot be kept if only one side has its heart in it.

When I am at Mass, Lord, I would hope to be passionate about your covenant. I watch the priest call upon your Spirit to bless and make the gifts holy. Let me see this as my self-gift, as a gift with and in you. Then send your Spirit upon me so that I go forth with a whole and holy heart.

≣ FOR REFLECTION

- Believers understand the new covenant in Christ to be in part behavioral and in part sacramental. The new covenant is in blood and, thus, in sacrifice and specifically in Eucharist. The living of it is presumed if one is a regular communicant and attentive to the proclamation of the Word. How do I deal with what is sometimes a big gap between our rituals and our wills?

- G.K. Chesterton is often named as the one who said that Christianity is not an experiment that failed but one that has yet, by and large, to be tried. Do I agree or disagree? How and why?

27 | WHEN DEAD SOULS CRY

➤ READ BARUCH 1–5

Open your eyes, O Lord, and see, for the dead who are in Hades, whose spirit has been taken from their bodies, will not ascribe glory or justice to the Lord; but the person who is deeply grieved, who walks bowed and feeble, with failing eyes and famished soul, will declare your glory and righteousness, O Lord. BARUCH 2:17–18

When we give God's law, God's prophets, and God's wisdom short shrift, there can be dire consequences. The Babylonian captivity was one of them.

Baruch, understood to have been a secretary or scribe to Jeremiah, recounts in his short book how some of those uprooted from their homeland realized that, "because of the wickedness of the house of Israel and the house of Judah," they had actually set themselves up. Echoing the Book of Lamentations, Baruch reflects on how ease, material comforts, and a lax spirit had made his people easy prey for the Chaldeans and King Nebuchadnezzar.

So the walls and dwellings of their holy city were in smithereens, and their glorious temple was destroyed. As a result, some of them awakened. That old description of them as a "stiff-necked people" cut them to the bone with its accuracy. The bull-headed don't listen. The bull-headed are impenetrable. No one can talk sense to them, and they tune out warning bells. Until.

Until the worst happens, and everything they have held dear is lost.

Jeremiah had warned them that replacing God with little gods and substituting little transgressions and petty crimes for observance would open doors wide for capital crime, infidelity, disaster, and captivity.

Both Lamentations and Baruch recount that some of the starving in Jerusalem had actually been reduced to eating their children. And these had been people who saw family and legacy as God's gift and the sign of their status as chosen people. But they had grown indolent, frivolous, and self-consumed. By then, they were beyond desperation.

Deadened souls, though, as long as there is some trace of life, can cry. Once they realize the truth of their situation and of themselves, their crying souls can rise. Once they lift up their heads and their hands, God bends as low as necessary to rescue them.

So, as Baruch tells it, those who had been on the edge of physical and spiritual death are refreshed by memories of the stories of God's ancient acts and the goodness of God's wisdom.

One of the great miracles of the spiritual life is that we can remember, we can come back, and that God's mercy is available even to the groveling and the guilty.

≋ PRAYER

Good God, your Holy Spirit continues to speak in us, even in the worst of times and even to the worst of us. Wake me up. Call me back with whatever it takes.

≋ FOR REFLECTION

- We are always dismayed by tales of human and urban wreckage and desecration of sacred places. Yet horrors take place. What do we make of human-wrought ruins? How can we repair them?

- We cringe when we hear of people cannibalizing their own children. Meanwhile, many nations, including our own, tolerate abortion and have high rates of child abuse and neglect. How on earth does that happen?

- What, in my own life, are the areas of laxity, self-indulgence, and indifference to crimes against life? Do I invite the Spirit in to direct and correct me?

28 | NEW HEART, NEW SPIRIT

◆ READ EZEKIEL 36

I will put my spirit within you, and make you follow my statutes and be careful to observe my ordinances. Then you shall live in the land I gave to your ancestors... EZEKIEL 36:27–28A

There's an ecological element to Ezekiel. Before he begins to speak of a new covenant that God proposes to make with Israel, he speaks of offenses to creation.

The enemies of Israel have pillaged and wasted. God instructs Ezekiel: "Therefore prophesy concerning the land of Israel, and say to the mountains and hills, to the watercourses and valleys, Thus says the Lord God: I am speaking in my jealous wrath, because you have suffered the insults of the nations" (Ezekiel 36:6). The prophet proceeds with God's warning that the consequences to the insulting nations would likewise be insults—and injury.

There is a sense that the land itself, with all its features and creatures, is a living system. If Psalms 104 and 148 can sing of non-human creation praising God, it stands to reason that Ezekiel envisions a world that can cry out when it suffers damages. The earth itself is spirited, since all of it has been breathed forth by the Spirit.

Perhaps, then, it is not far-fetched to suggest that the repatriation and cleansing that God promises Israel also is intended for the land. The new heart and new spirit God gives are positioned to bring abundance and beauty.

This new covenant is an all-around restoration. The people are glad and honor God even while they are simply relieved to be home. The fields flourish and the water is pure. The flocks bounce and flounce around the meadows. The trees are heavy with fruit.

One of the startling remarks that occurs in the midst of this pastoral picture-painting is this: "It is not for your sake that I will act, says the Lord God." God follows with a scolding smack at the people.

It is not just the enemies who have plundered and laid waste. So the new covenant is conditioned on the reverence and upright living of the people Israel. This includes a renewal of their primal charge to "till and keep" the garden (Genesis 2:15).

This new covenant, a boon to the people, is for the sake of what the Spirit intended in those first waves of wind. The covenant Ezekiel announces is for God's sake. It is for the sake of the Spirit-filled earth and for the Holy Land too.

≡ PRAYER

God our Maker, inspire in me a spirit that sees the living and non-living world around me as family. As you renew me, make me a good companion of all creation.

≡ FOR REFLECTION

- In *Laudato Si'*, Pope Francis sets forth a comprehensive vision of ecological responsibility. Along with urges for action, he delineates an ecological spirituality. How would I characterize such a spirituality? How do I live it in a practical way? Where am I falling short?

29 | BONES AND BONES AND DRY BONES

≡ **READ EZEKIEL 37:1-14**

Thus says the Lord God to these bones: I will cause breath to enter you, and you shall live. I will lay sinews on you, and will cause flesh to come upon you, and cover you with skin, and put breath in you, and you shall live... EZEKIEL 37:5-6

From time to time, walkers in the tall pine tracts of North Carolina and South Carolina come upon bones in the pine straw. These typically are bones of deer or squirrels or the occasional rabbit. Down at the southern tip of South Carolina, closer to Savannah, there can also be remnants of the armor of armadillos and lifeless turtle shells. Turkey vultures and buzzards make short work of pecking and yanking away every trace of skin and meat.

Ezekiel's vision in the valley was far more grisly and unnatural than the findings of hikers. It would be more comparable to the Allies going into Hitler's concentration camps or Poles discovering the truth of the massacres wrought by Stalin's Soviets at Katyn.

Dead bones, we know, do nothing but dry and crumble. Eventually they become a bit of powder and salt in the dust, soft and soil-like as the reddish brown stuff that sifts through the fingers if one scoops it from the stump of a rotted fallen tree.

We are made of matter, but we are ultimately immaterial. To be more than a mix of calcium, phosphorus, iron, and magnesium, we need food and water. We need muscle, cartilage, and strength. We need blood running in blue streams just under our skin and flushing red when released into air. And for all that we need spirit in the form of breath.

Ezekiel reminds us that we are really as good as dead, really a cache of dry bones if there is no spirit in us. For the breath to come to those piles of human bones, Ezekiel is told to invoke the four winds. Getting flesh and sinew and bone functional is a cooperative effort.

The fact that we live at all is evidence of interdependence. We depend on wind and weather, fresh air and clean water, life that we can hug tight and life that we can eat. We depend on the God that we call First Cause and Prime Mover.

Nothing does anything without mutuality and the synchronicity of mineral life, vegetable life, animal life, human life, and spirit life. Ezekiel's vision was no hallucination. It was simply a life story, a basic lesson in biology and religion.

≡ PRAYER

Father, Son, and Spirit, pull all of me together—with all around me too. Let these bones live.

≡ FOR REFLECTION

- In the introduction to his massive three-volume work, *I Believe in the Holy Spirit*, Yves Congar refers to his life as a combined vocation of intellect and affect. He presents himself as a person who does profound theological study and also devoutly prays. He offers his work to his readers with this hope: "The Spirit is breath. The wind sings in the trees. I would like, then, to be an Aeolian harp and let the breath of God make the strings vibrate and sing. Let me stretch and tune the strings—that will be the austere task of research. And then let the Spirit make them sing a clear and tuneful song of prayer and life!" (Congar, x). If I were to sum up my life-work and my life of prayer, how would I express it? What would I hope to send forth into the world from my living bones?

30 | WISDOM'S RELAY

≋ **READ DANIEL 2**

> *"Blessed be the name of God from age to age, for wisdom and power are his...[H]e gives wisdom to the wise and knowledge to those who have understanding."* DANIEL 2:20–21

The prophet Daniel, always a figure of virtue and intelligence, suggests that there's a divine relay at play. God *has* wisdom and power. God gives wisdom to people who can grasp it. There are those who *do get* it. Then Daniel, a loyal God-fearer and a good human learner, is one of those who *receives, with their help,* God's wisdom. And, of course, he *passes it on.*

So it goes from God to a collection of competent, pious humans to Daniel to those with whom he shares it. We know the stories of his canny interpretation of kings' dreams and writing on a wall. We also know what fidelity got him tossed into the lion's den. It's as if to say wise people may translate the cryptic but also end up as potential foodstuff for ravenous beasts.

Daniel was smarter than temptation and persecution. His God proved to be more powerful than treacherous, insecure monarchs.

What if things had not played out that way, though? The visionary Book of Daniel used the term "Son of Man," and we know that Jesus applied that term to himself. Jesus, too, displayed an exceptional ability to read hearts, minds, cycles of seasons, weather, threats, and the signs of the times. To Jesus, St. Paul applied the term "sophia," wisdom, the prime attribute of the Spirit. He also suffered death by crucifixion as a result of his wisdom.

Biblical wisdom builds a house and holds a banquet, as Proverbs has it. God has showered down wisdom's goods. Humans accept or reject those goods. They invite others to share them. There are those, however, who prefer applejack and moonshine to wisdom's wine, and burgers and fries to her delicacies. There are those who opt for stupidity over learning and falsehood over truth. Sometimes, when they are confronted with obstacles or challenges to their comfort, they prefer murder to reason.

The fact that such things happen doesn't deter the wise from rising and imparting their wisdom. The Holy Spirit impels them, after all.

Daniel mentions that the wisdom given to him in that relay has also come with power. It is actually the power handed off straight from God.

And it keeps coming, often in the most unlikely ways.

≡ PRAYER

Remind me, God, that I count on your Spirit to be with me in all situations. Thus, I am not intimidated. Make me confident and strong, even in the presence of those who can dictate my fate.

≡ FOR REFLECTION

- While Daniel lived long and outlived several kings, we tend to focus on stories of his youth. How might Daniel and his companions be held up as role models, even to those young people who have never known kings and cannot imagine dens of lions or fiery furnaces? What current threats resemble those that these ancient young people faced?

- What situations and what persons are likely to intimidate me? How do I overcome that fear, and what am I willing to pay if I offend or cross them?

31 | FOOL AND MADMAN?

Israel cries, "The prophet is a fool, the man of the spirit is mad!"
Because of your great iniquity, your hostility is great.

HOSEA 9:7

Amid prosperity, who wants to be told that there's a sickness in society? The prophet Hosea denounced idolatry, what he called "whoredom," and the semblances of success that succored a false confidence.

Really, who wants to be informed about lackadaisical priests and ho-hum religionists, faithless leaders and contentedly ignorant citizens, and, on top of that or at the bottom of it all, a duplicitous public committing a list of crimes and sins that will end in crumbling walls and sacked treasures? Any and all of the above, or any references to them, are marvelous ear-closers. The fact is that we prefer chicken-in-every-pot political slogans and Wall Street and Nikkei reports that seduce us into believing that we are on the high road. Prestige and affluence are our birthright, we believe. And we're unassailable.

So anyone who is standing up and insisting that things are in disarray and that our presumptions are wrong-headed tends to be written off as a malcontent. Those who go raving in the streets are probably off their meds, we surmise. It's the Chicken Little phenomenon, we're pretty sure. We dismiss their predictions of eco-disasters and name those who sniff out corporate or governmental corruption not watchdogs but wolf criers. It's easier not to listen to them.

Hosea suffered that social problem. Even the drama of his prostitute wife and his own extraordinary faithfulness and tenderness, even the cries of God—for which he served as a mouthpiece—didn't seem to merit much attention. Hosea's declamations were blown off.

We sing his "Come back to me" hymn. Occasionally we buy leather-covered, gilt-edged editions of the book in which he and his words appear. But we would rather not consider the possibility that his social analyses of the situation of Israel in the eighth century B.C. have relevance to us.

We don't expect the Spirit to compare our world to Hosea's. We think we are so advanced and so beyond all that.

Dear God, Hosea calls us into the desert tenderly and out of our comfort harshly. Let me listen, Lord, knowing that your Spirit intends to speak to me through the prophet's words. They may be old, but you guarantee that for me, for us, they are always living.

≡ **FOR REFLECTION**

- Prophetic figures and those who critique civil society tend to be rejected. All sorts of attempts are made to discredit them and muffle their voices. As I think about the lives of Peter Maurin and Dorothy Day, what insights and works of theirs have proved to be viable and truly inspired? How do I account for the fact that they and the Catholic Worker movement were less than appreciated by church members and leaders for much of their lives?

- Can I identify some contemporary voices that seem to be prophetic, even if a bit unusual? How do I know the prophets from the cranks?

32 | OUTPOURING POSSIBILITY

🗏 **READ JOEL 2**

Then afterward I will pour out my spirit on all flesh; your sons and your daughters shall prophesy, your old men shall dream dreams, and your young men shall see visions. Even on the male and female slaves, in those days, I will pour out my spirit. JOEL 2:28–29

Prophets see through. Dreamers see possibility. Visionaries see things above and sometimes things to come.

When Joel speaks of the outpouring of the Holy Spirit on citizens and slaves alike, he is presuming a people who have responded positively to God's invitation to return with their whole hearts. Joel envisions a comeback of beauty and bounty. Reversing Isaiah, he calls upon the people to "Beat your plowshares into swords, and your pruning hooks into spears" (Joel 3:10). Amid restoration, then, Joel fully expects a spirited battle to ensue. We honestly don't know whether he anticipates bloodshed or whether he is using military imagery to forecast decisive spiritual combat.

There is much about our world and God's providence that we don't understand. The late archbishop of Mexico City, Luis Martinez, wrote: "The providential designs of God are hidden in human events. On one day, the last day of the world, and eternally in Heaven, we shall contemplate the full meaning of human history. Now we see things—such as the reason for war, for catastrophes, for all the tremendous vicissitudes of history—in fragmentary and imperfect manner" (*True Devotion*, 194). The plans of God and the glimpses we get into the meaning of contemporary events come only with two things: 1) time, particularly the endtime, and 2) the Holy Spirit's gift of understanding.

Even the prophecies, dreams, and visions we see, the ones deemed genuine and true, remain incomplete. They help us see to the horizon but don't carry us beyond it. Or they help us peer down to the rocky or shell strewn bottom of a bay but only in shallow water. We know that the clouds or the sun or the eastern horizon line are coming from somewhere else. We perceive that the sandy bottom slopes down and down and down the farther we go out, and the unaided eye cannot begin to see what coral structures or oddly configured fish may be there. We need, on the one hand, flight and fuel. On the other, we need tanks of air and diving gear and light.

The Holy Spirit draws us simply to come back, to come closer, to revel in blessings, to assent to the little we understand, and to arm ourselves against those who would pull us away. We can trust in God-made promises of marvelous future possibility. But it takes our capacity to see beyond temporalities and petty self-interest to realize those outpouring promises.

⫸ PRAYER

Pour out on me, Holy Spirit, the graces and gifts of a heaven-bent world. Equip me for flight and for depth, for fight and for bliss. Above all, let me see and dream and live what your visions reveal.

⫸ FOR REFLECTION

- Utopia is what we want. Generally speaking, utopian visions and utopian communities come and go—often very quickly. The Shakers are a good American example. However, other ideals of better ways do last. What are some examples of communal living projects that have stood the test of time? Have I visited any such places?

- Old and young, the privileged and the slave, are among those on whom Joel says the Spirit will be poured out. Why is it so important that believers have a deeply egalitarian vision? Where can I do something concrete to alleviate the effects of prejudice and to celebrate those who tend to be overlooked?

- What hidden dreams need a real Christmas to unwrap them?

Selected

NEW
TESTAMENT

Readings

33 | ANNUNCIATION

⇛ **READ LUKE 1:26-38**

The angel said to her, "The Holy Spirit will come upon you, and the power of the Most High will overshadow you; therefore the child to be born will be holy; he will be called Son of God." LUKE 1:35

One of the most memorable paintings of the Annunciation hangs in the nineteenth-century American gallery of the Philadelphia Museum of Art. It is Henry Osawa Tanner's beige, buff, off-white, yellow, brown depiction of a girl who looks to be the age of an eighth or ninth grader. She is seated on a propped mat of a bed, and material with the look of a traditional Hebrew prayer shawl is close at hand. She appears to be shy, tentative, and perhaps a bit stymied but also alert and reflective. Tanner, the son of an African American preacher, spent decades in Paris, so the influences of the impressionists are evident. Gabriel is shown simply as a wide column of light. The incandescence seems to come from within.

We know the story. Mary gets the message and invitation and gives her *Fiat* without quite knowing how all this will work out and what it might mean. She is told that she will be made a mother and simply that God will accomplish it.

There was no treasure map that prepared a hunter for this event, no cloud she or anyone was awaiting on the horizon, no mountain to ascend, no bush to approach, no wilderness into which she was to retreat, no dovecote to enter. Mary says yes, and the overshadowing somehow, on some timetable, happens. We're inclined to believe that the conceiving was instantaneous.

When we meditate on this event, we tend to play miracle music in our imaginations and to make it all quite pretty. We don't consider the maiden's probable confusion, and we barely reflect on the consternation of the parents and Joseph. We may just think—on March 25, say—oh, hooray, only nine months till Christmas.

But there's more.

Spiritual writers and the saints of the centuries have reflected on

Mary's sinlessness and her absolute submission of mind and heart. They have named her God-bearer and argued until the Council of Ephesus (431 A.D.) as to whether she ought rightly be called Mother of God.

We are left to wonder what it might have been like to have the growing Christ Child, a divine fetus, gathering cells for muscle and blood and bone within her.

Father Gary Caster, a campus minister and leader of parish missions, notes the frequent Marian themes: contemplation, self-gift, freedom. But he also draws our attention to the fact that for all the months of pregnancy Mary had the Body of Christ within her. Bone of her bone, flesh of her flesh, body and blood.

As Caster says, "Every dimension of her person resonates with the connection she now shares with Christ. This is precisely what it means to have the Holy Spirit in one's life" (Caster, 53).

We, who have been fully initiated into the faith, sometimes become quite blasé. Familiarity doesn't breed contempt, but it can beget complacency. We forget that we have been and are overshadowed by the Holy Spirit. We forget that our mission every minute of every day is somehow to bear Christ to the world. We forget that every Holy Communion unites us, all of our vulnerable and tainted being, with the Body and Blood, Soul and Divinity of Christ. He is in us as much as he was in the expectant Mary.

So we must remember to tread surely but lightly en route to our Elizabeths and Zechariahs and imminent Baptizers, whoever they are in our lives.

⬚ PRAYER

I pray the Angelus: *"And the Word was made flesh and dwelt among us." Come, Holy Spirit, so that the divine Word may dwell again in us, in me.*

⬚ FOR REFLECTION

- What are my favorite images of the Blessed Virgin? Is there a particular depiction of the Annunciation that moves me? Where have I seen it?

- How do I imagine that Mary understood the working of the Holy Spirit in her life and especially in her pregnancy?

34 | THE CHILD FROM WHERE?

READ MATTHEW 1:18-25

Before they lived together, she was found to be with child from the Holy Spirit. MATTHEW 1:18B

Right after the long, unpronounceable genealogy that opens Matthew's gospel, the shaken Joseph is introduced as a good and gentle man who wants to spare Mary "public disgrace." At first, it almost seems as if he has wished that God would provide a paternity test. He clearly knows the child is not his. Just in time, an angel confirms what the text has just said: that Mary's child is "from the Holy Spirit." There is no explanation of how or why this should be so, but Joseph is told the child will save his people.

We immediately can assume several things about Joseph from this brief account. These things instruct us about what sanctity—the real spirited life—looks like. First, Joseph is a prudent man who is fair-minded and presumably prayerful. He wants to handle this awkward situation delicately. Second, he is neither vindictive nor tied to the letter of the law or its most dire prescriptions for punishment. He is obviously an observant Jew, but he does not think that death by stoning is the way to deal with an adulterous woman (as he must have initially presumed Mary was) or her unborn child. Third, he trusts and obeys, even when the guidance comes from an apparition. There is something within him that recognizes and assents to the dream-vision of an angel and the direction that angel gives him.

Only a free person could do that. Much later, when St. Paul speaks of the freedom bestowed on the Christian, he could have pointed to the Blessed Virgin and St. Joseph as models. Extraordinary events, sprung from extraordinary requests, open the way to a whole new phase of salvation history. Only free, confident people can deal with such events with composure.

Interestingly enough, the freedom of Joseph and Mary is their freedom to be attentive to the core of God's law and faithful to the promise

HOLY WIND, HOLY FIRE

of the prophets. It is also a freedom to be true and faithful to themselves. Saints have to hold a self-possession that propels them through mission, adventure, and trial. They must be free to grasp what is truly "from the Holy Spirit," even if they have no DNA or chemical analyses, no touchstones, no karat assaying, no witnesses, no recordings, no public documents for verification. The holy sometimes just know.

Deep down, where holy things come from, they find assurance and peace. Even without clear explanations.

⇛ PRAYER

Blessed St. Joseph, you made a home for the Messiah and his Blessed Mother. Care for our homes and provide for us too. Be a model for fathers and workers. Let us take you as a guide assuring us that truly brave men are gentle and holy and Spirit-led.

⇛ FOR REFLECTION

- There are superstitions about St. Joseph (such as planting statues in the yard when one wants to sell a house). There are also devotions and lovely hymns. Yet Joseph has always been seen as the most silent of major figures in the action of the New Testament. What can we surmise and what can we be sure of in regard to this foster father of the Lord?

- Along with the Solemnity of St. Joseph celebrated on March 19, the church also offers a liturgy of St. Joseph the Worker on May 1. The latter originated as a counter to the famed May Day parades displaying Soviet weapons and troops. Americans might prefer now to celebrate St. Joseph on Labor Day. Whatever the timing, why is it important to celebrate Joseph? And why has the church recently inserted his name into the Eucharistic prayers in the Roman Missal?

35 | IN MOTION

⇒ **READ LUKE 1:39–56**

When Elizabeth heard Mary's greeting, the child leaped in her womb.
And Elizabeth was filled with the Holy Spirit...   LUKE 1:41

A large red cylindrical plastic can, toppled in a yard, can look, from a distance, like the hunched form of a red-shirted gardener bent over mulch. As one gets closer and the 20/20 kicks in, it becomes clear that there is nothing moving.

Movement, of course, is the telltale life sign, even if it's only the movement of a sleeping person's breathing. Or perhaps it's that leaping in the womb, the baby kick that is noted as Mary approaches the threshold of Elizabeth's home in Ain Karim.

St. Thomas Aquinas noted that anything that moves has a kind of soul. Thus, there are vegetative souls, animal souls, and rational souls. As human beings, we celebrate movement and change in so many ways that we can never number them.

We pencil lines on walls to watch children's height climb. We monitor babies and heart function and brain activity with sonograms, electroencephalograms, EKGs, and a steady stream of new devices. We strap on gadgets to count our daily footsteps. We track auto mileage with odometers, and we use treadmills to up our pace. We flex and stretch and sprint and swim and skate and dance and lift and bend and hammer nails and stir whatever is cooking from dawn to dusk. We sometimes fancy that we're Olympians. After all, it's possible that we've ascended some godly mountains in our days.

But we have to recall that our pep and strength have a source. The breath of life entered the first human and thus a living person came to be. Pulse and beat become our being too, and at birth we shift from prenatal swim to gulping in air with our first good cry. The Spirit, of course, is the one we understand and proclaim in our Creed as life-giver, vivifier.

When we're spirited, we move. When we're holy spirited, we greet the God within and the God outside. We recognize God's gift, and we declare ourselves ready to welcome or overcome whatever is about to happen. We give our consent to being part of the plan. And we hasten and open our arms as friends of God leap.

≋ PRAYER

Spirit of God, help me to recognize the presence of the Lord wherever and whenever he shows up. And move me.

≋ FOR REFLECTION

- How do I imagine this scene of the Visitation playing out? Is there anything in it I can apply to my own life of family loyalty, care for elders, and joy at the announcement of a pregnancy?

- Elizabeth is "filled with the Holy Spirit." In the charismatic renewal, many people who have received the baptism in the Spirit (a praying over, not sacramental baptism or confirmation) attest to having been filled by the Spirit. What would that be like? Have I experienced moments when I have been aware of being filled with the Spirit?

*Then, opening their treasure chests, they offered him gifts of gold,
frankincense, and myrrh. And having been warned in a dream not to
return to Herod, they left for their own country by another road. Now
after they had left, an angel of the Lord appeared to Joseph in a dream
and said, "Get up, take the child and his mother, and flee to Egypt..."*

MATTHEW 2:11–13

They pop up four times in the first two chapters of Matthew. Joseph
learns how to respond to Mary's pregnancy, then, after the birth of Jesus,
heeds the warning to flee the country, and then, after Herod's death,
knows it is time to go back to Israel—all because of dreams. The wise
men, previously star gazers, greet and gift the Christ Child and then get
the message to go back to the East by a different route—the outcome of
a dream or dreams.

Dream analysts tell us all sorts of things, some spot-on, others dubi-
ous. They say our dreams are the prompts of our unconscious. The problem is that we don't generally have access to that, and we don't know
whether the posited collective unconscious actually exists. Another
more plausible theory is that our dreams are a kind of soup of memories, daydreams, fragmentary experiences and observations, and sublim-
inal messages that turn into a stew of creative nonfiction, a fictionalized
memoir, or a futuristic novel partially based on fact. Another spin on
the interpretation of dreams claims that if there are three characters in a
dream, each one represents some aspect of ourselves.

If these ideas are true, then we would have to say that Joseph and
the Magi tapped into their own unconscious for insight into looming
events and intuitively read God's mind. They perhaps had picked up the
rumblings of a whole culture that knew—collectively—that Herod was
a madman and serial killer. Joseph certainly, and the Magi perhaps, knew
the ancient story of the murderous Pharaoh of Moses' time, and the

story may have impelled the sense of urgency in their dreams. If, in fact, three characters appeared in their dreams, they clearly did not include the mad king. None of the group, Joseph or the Magi, had about them any traces of the greed, sensuality, blood thirstiness, and paranoia of that sell-out monarch. If they dreamed of angels, Mary, Moses, or some other forebears, or even of each other, it is reasonable to assume that they had something of the character of these within them.

All of us can attest that some dreams are just plain zany, and some are riddled with remnants of screenplay—cinematic, televised, or computer-generated. Joseph and the Magi lived in a simpler (which is not to say easier) world. They did not have all the visual stimuli that can sometimes play into our dreams.

They could see star-studded intergalactic skies clearly. Which may have made their dreams more trustworthy. In any case, they had the good sense to know that sometimes God's Spirit speaks to the human heart and mind in sleep.

≋ PRAYER

Spirit of goodness, Spirit of peace, make me both dreamer and doer. Help me to be faithful to God's plan for my life, and help me be protective of God's plans for the lives of others.

≋ FOR REFLECTION

- One popular director of retreats used to say that maybe we should have another Joseph feast besides March 19 and May 1. He suggested that we call it the feast of St. Joseph the Snoozer. His point was that St. Joseph and the Magi too exemplify these lesser known verses from the Psalms: "It is in vain that you rise up early and go late to rest, eating the bread of anxious toil; for he gives sleep to his beloved" (Psalm 127:2). How can we distinguish God-inspired dreams from ones that are just a weave of fancy and whim?

37 | WATER AND WILDERNESS

≋ **READ MARK 1:4-13**

And the Spirit immediately drove him out into the wilderness. He was in the wilderness forty days, tempted by Satan; and he was with the wild beasts... MARK 1:12-13

A trip to the Shipe orchards on Old Furnace Road outside Danville, Pennsylvania, will reveal one of the precious secrets of cider-making. As the farmhands tell it, there are loads of sweet, unwormholed, unbruised apples that go into the cider press. But they make uninteresting cider if they're left alone. You have to add a select number of rotten apples to the mash to get tang and a bit of fizz. Cider made without those rotten apples is just plain dull. It's baby-taste apple juice.

Somehow that makes sense of the baptism and the desert tempta-tion of Christ. The sweetness of the event was his very unnecessary pre-senting of himself for baptism. It was a baptism of repentance, after all, and Jesus had nothing to repent. Adding to the sweetness of the circum-stance was the descent of the Holy Spirit and the voice from above pro-claiming the Father's good pleasure.

The rottenness showed up when the Spirit drove Jesus into the wil-derness and allowed him to be served temptation after temptation. Add to that mix a collection of wild beasts loitering there.

Somehow the messianic mission and ministry of Jesus needed not only a divine seal of approval, unholed and unbruised. It also needed the zing added by a confrontation with Satan and with snarling company.

Perhaps we too find that the apple cider of our lives has matured as we have faced setbacks, snide remarks, hurts, snubs, heartbreak, illness, accidents, and outsized temptations. For us to mature in virtue, we need along the way to have met and mixed with a lot of unsavory vices—the wild beasts of culture and the potential wild beast in us. Jesus came back from the wilderness and ate with sinners. He understood something of what drove them, even though he had never given into it. The Spirit saw to it that the bad apples got in the mash. Later Jesus would aver that those exactly were the ones he came to save.

Rotten apples don't remain merely rotten in cider. They are converted into something luscious, especially when warmed on a chilly fall night.

In the desert, amid the temptations and the fanged and clawed things that Jesus faced, "the angels waited on him." The good spirits are always close at hand. Because of that, we recognize as Friend the one who knows both sides of things when we bring our often contradictory and mixed-up selves to worship. And we are equipped to choose—to become cider.

⇛ PRAYER

Guiding Spirit, give me confidence in the nearness of angels and good companions. But give me, too, comfort with the broken and bruised, with all their shortcomings. Give me maturity and resignation to a world that only works with weeds and wheat, rotten and sweet.

⇛ FOR REFLECTION

- Throughout the history of Christendom, the followers of the Lord have stepped into dangerous places. What is it about us that tends to take risks? Is there a risk to our souls, in the sense that we might find ourselves joining rather than beating wrongdoing? How do we fend off that risk without abandoning the places where we have been called?

- Who or what might be the unsavory characters, the tempters, or the wild beasts that I might have to confront while evangelizing?

38 | WATER AND SPIRIT

🕮 **READ JOHN 3:1-21**

> Jesus answered, "Very truly, I tell you, no one can enter the kingdom of
> God without being born of water and the Spirit. What is born of flesh
> is flesh, and what is born of Spirit is spirit…The wind blows where
> it chooses, and you hear the sound of it, but you do not know where
> it comes from or where it goes. So it is of everyone who is born of the
> Spirit." JOHN 3:5–6, 8

Alice Walker, Chris Offutt, and Ted Moroney are among those who
have produced books entitled *The Same River Twice*. A docudrama by
the same name stunned audiences at the Sundance Film Festival. The
title always has an ironic twist to it. The saying from which the oft-re-
peated title is borrowed denies that there is any such thing as a same
river. Heraclitus, way back in the sixth century before Christ, observed
that it is simply impossible to step into the same river twice. The one
constant is change, and water itself, though it always has the same molec-
ular makeup, moves, pools, seeps, and washes.

We know that Jesus used the image of living water as a self-referent.
He himself was offering it. For him, living water meant fresh water, water
that was not stagnant, water that could cleanse and quench. In surroundings where John's practice of baptizing in the Jordan was known, the
water Jesus spoke of suggested something even fresher. True, it harked
back to the crossing into the Promised Land. But it also seemed to say
something more. Jesus was offering a refreshment and a stepping into
mystery, a new exodus, an entry into promise. Water and Spirit would be
power-sources for refreshment and redirection. The disciples would find
that even when floods seemed to sweep everything away, they opened
up a fine newness.

Poets have long personified water. Brooks babble, streams soothe,
mountain lakes rest serenely, and seas can rage. Water, because of its
fluidity, signals movement and change. Whether a creek sways gently

through woodlands and meadows or a tide mounts at moonrise, we sense vitality and power in water. Our human bodies are, after all, 60% to 70% water. Our liveliness, our living spirit, relies on water.

When Jesus recommends baptism in water and the Spirit as the sluiceway to the kingdom of heaven, we can imagine that he is urging us to flow forth, to move with the wind and respond to the gravitational pull that promises to merge us with all manner of tributaries pouring into a majestic bay.

God adopts us in baptism but has loved us all along. That's what we find when we become part of the watershed. Baptismal water splashes briefly, but it changes everything. And so, not surprisingly, warm morning showers, slim streams of water seeping through bamboo pipe into an artful Japanese tea garden, clarinet contemplation, kind words, and soft whispers of thanks and praise and mercy flow. They shape and remake the river of our being.

And we find, by the grace of God, that we can't step into the same selves twice.

≋ PRAYER

God of graceful flow and change, I don't ask magic of your Spirit or your sacraments. I do, though, believe you transform the world and me in mysterious and unseen ways. Help me to be one who calms and beautifies and offers wellsprings of peace. Let the water of my eyes clear and see. Let the water of my heart flow happily. Let the water of my mind awaken to kind days. And may my word and works help restructure our world.

≋ FOR REFLECTION

- What do I understand to be the effects of baptism? How do I account for the fact that baptism cleanses us of original sin and yet the inclination and capacity to sin remains in us? How do I keep awash in goodness and diminish the undertow of evil?

39 | LIVING RIVER

READ John 7:37–44

On the last day of the festival…, [Jesus]cried out, "Let anyone who is thirsty come to me, and let the one who believes in me drink. As the scripture has said, 'Out of the believer's heart shall flow rivers of living water.'" Now he said this about the Spirit, which believers in him were to receive. JOHN 7:37–39

Quite possibly, quite plausibly, the Holy Spirit bubbles up less often like a geyser and more often like a water fountain. A geyser shoots, sky high and mightily, from rock fissures and rough soil. It's strong and steady, a release of vaulting, concentrated pressure. A water fountain, however, takes some turn of hand. Its water is available, but it can be stopped and stored.

The Holy Spirit is assuredly a strong and irrepressible force, always operant. That is the Spirit that is life breath, good tug, world turn, all unseen. But our experience cranks the Spirit's evidence with our thirst. We twist on with prayer, off with forgetfulness, on with urgency, off with our relentless settings aside for whatever now distracts us. We want the Spirit present in our dry spells of tedious decisions, relational doubts, job quests, and all manner of ironings out. Once we're not so needy (or at least not consciously so) we tend to forget that there is a Holy Spirit yearning to be freed.

What we need, though, is a holy thirst that suffices to get our attention. Even if it's only a squirt, we need that refreshment that recalls to us that the world is geyser-rich. And that refreshment, too, must recall to us that we ourselves have the capacity not only to drink but to be living river.

Since I have received you, Spirit, let your rivers flow in me. Help me bring refreshment and relief to those around me who thirst. Make me the one who asks first what I can do for them.

≣ **FOR REFLECTION**

- What parches me? What are my best sources of spiritual refreshment?

- When do I find that I can be a source of spiritual refreshment for others? How do I know what to do and when to do it? Am I more like a geyser or a spigot?

40 | SPIRIT SPEECH

⇒ **READ MARK 13:9-13**

"When they bring you to trial and hand you over, do not worry beforehand about what you are to say, but say whatever is given to you at that time, for it is not you who speak but the Holy Spirit." MARK 13:11

For a while there, blithe believers thought the age of martyrs was over, maybe with Hitler and Stalin. But since El Salvador—Romero, the sisters, the Maryknoll lay missionary, the Jesuits, their housekeeper, her daughter—and Sister Dorothy Stang in Brazil, we've understood that Christians pose a threat to dictators, guerrillas, and those who oppress both the poor and the land.

Since the school shootings of the 1990s and 2000s, beginning with Columbine, we've learned that teachers and students can be executed for unfathomable reasons or none at all. Some of them have been asked, before fatal gunfire, whether they were Christians. Some of them were never asked a thing.

Since the rise of the Taliban, al-Qaeda, and ISIS, we have known too that people can be blown apart or beheaded or run down by a truck irrespective of anything other than their participation in secular society. Or they can have their throats slit in a small village church because they are at morning Mass.

From the earliest days, Christians have been tortured and killed. Christ and we ourselves seem to be gravely offensive to the social order and people's stolid beliefs.

If and when it should happen that we're called to witness, the Lord has promised we will be given what to say. By and in the Holy Spirit, we will know when to be silent (Jesus was) and when to speak (Jesus did).

The nineteenth-century evangelist Charles Spurgeon has observed that the Holy Spirit as Comforter is loving, faithful, safe, active, and successful (Spurgeon, 13-19). The Spirit, in other words, is a reliable love, one pledged never to abandon us, a refuge in distress and relaxer when we surrender our agitation. The Spirit is involved and provides. The Holy Spirit does good deeds—for us, in us, through us.

The Holy Spirit is also a witherer (Spurgeon, 81-100) insofar as the Spirit confronts falsehood, injustice, oppression, and weaknesses of the flesh. The withering look or dead stare from the witherer is what discomfits the killers.

That same withering Spirit stands tall in us—which explains why the narratives of martyrs and their martyrdoms always show them to have been steady, strong, and sure.

⇒ PRAYER

Spirit of God, help me to know when I need comforting and when I need withering. Also keep me ready and alert for times when I may be called on to defend my faith or simply to declare that I have and hold it.

⇒ FOR REFLECTION

- What stories of martyrs or the past have inspired me? Do I have any favorite among the martyrs of the early church?

- What martyrs of less affluent countries am I familiar with? Do I know stories of recent martyrs? Can I picture myself having the courage to die for persons, causes, or faith?

41 | THE UNFORGIVABLE SIN

➤ **READ MARK 3:28–29**; ALSO SEE **MATTHEW 12:31–32** OR **LUKE 12:10**

"Truly I tell you, people will be forgiven for their sins and whatever blasphemies they utter; but whoever blasphemes against the Holy Spirit can never have forgiveness, but is guilty of an eternal sin." MARK 3:28–29

Right after talk about the fact that one cannot break into the home of a strong man and carry off all his portable goods without first binding up that strong man, Jesus launches into a paradoxical comment.

Amidst all of his talk of repentance and forgiveness, he says there is something absolutely unforgivable. The explanation usually given is often twofold. First, the blasphemy against the Spirit does not seem to be anything someone says. Rather, it seems to be refusal to accept grace—a definitive and defiant stance, a solid determination to stay unrepentant. Second, the blasphemy against the Spirit is sometimes thought of as final despair—a person's decision to resist the weight of revelation and conclude that one's own sinfulness is too great for God to forgive. It's a choice that denies God's mercy and omnipotence.

Both of these are related, of course. We can be dead set that no one can tell us something is wrong or that we have been in the wrong. Even when there is evidence that we *are* the ones who are wrong, we can reject that. We can slap grace in the face. We can just prefer not to choose God and the good. We can decide that no voices but the shady ones know what they are talking about.

We can also be convinced that we have been wrong and done wrong and are, as a result, unlovable and unforgivable. We figure that a self-respecting God would not want anything to do with us.

These are dark places to be. One is stuffed with ego. The other is crushed in mire. These are issues of hope and the abandonment of it, but they are also issues of faith. One cannot receive forgiveness and the refreshment of the Holy Spirit if he or she considers it not needed or impossible. Both positions are types of idolatry. One is built of narcissism. The other believes in a weak God, a God who can't abide our human muck.

Pablo Neruda, the Chilean poet, achieved youthful acclaim with *Twenty Love Poems and a Song of Despair*. In this little collection, he painted a picture of despair. In "The Light Wraps You," he described a mourner at twilight as the "pure heir of the ruined day." The young poet's writings were not by any means about the spiritual life, but they were portraiture of the emotional landscape of love lost and the feeling that the end of a romance is a wrecking ball that has undone a day, a life, all hope and heritage. In "The Song of Despair," he compared the depths of despair to a kind of tsunami in which everything is swamped and "swallowed" and left sodden and sunken (W.S. Merwin translation of Neruda, Penguin Books, 5, 83).

Something in the human spirit wants to climb out of or be rescued from these depths. Neruda lived to be a diplomat, a political activist, and Nobel prize winner. He did not remain in dark, dank places. He saw reasons to live—and lived passionately.

That's something the Holy Spirit invites us to as well—passionate life, here and for all eternity. We remain free, however, to prefer our own inner Alcatraz and to tamp down the sounds of any bird that sings.

≡ **PRAYER**
Spirit of God, let me never fall into that black hole of the soul that denies who you are and what you do and inflates the shadow of myself. Keep me looking up in hope.

≡ **FOR REFLECTION**
- We really don't know what final despair is like and with whom it may have occurred. Are there any historical incidents that make me suspect that someone or a group of people succumbed to that kind of despair?

- St. John of the Cross and St. Teresa of Kolkata are among those who experienced spiritual darkness. How would their dark nights of the soul differ from the sin against the Spirit?

42 | SYMBOL AND JOB DESCRIPTION

READ JOHN 14:25-30; AND **15:26—16:15**

"But the Advocate, the Holy Spirit, whom the Father will send in my name, will teach you everything, and remind you of all that I have said to you." JOHN 14:26

There is no way to explain the Holy Spirit, just as there is no way to define God or talk about the logic of the Trinity and its unity. When we speak of the Holy Spirit, we revert to symbols and manifestations and then consider what the role or mission of the Third Person of the One God might be.

The *Catechism of the Catholic Church* enumerates the many symbols customarily associated with the Spirit. Language and art, based on Scriptural scenes, display wind, fire, dove, water, oil of anointing, royal seal, finger of God's hand, and so on. But we notice that none of these quite tells the story. The prophet Elijah encounters the spirit of God in something like a whispering sound or a gentle breeze or, as the NRSV has it, in silence. At Jesus' baptism the Spirit hovers in the form of a dove. At Pentecost, we hear that the Spirit descends as something like a mighty wind and appears in tongues "as of" fire.

To use a slang expression, we find that even the authors of the inspired word find themselves talking about the phenomenon of the Spirit in "sort of like" terms. In the Nicene Creed, we profess our belief in "the Holy Spirit, the Lord, the giver of life, who proceeds from the Father and the Son, who with the Father and the Son is adored and glorified, who has spoken through the prophets." The symbols aren't here. Immediately we continue our list of beliefs. We believe in the church with its four marks, and in baptism and penance, the resurrection of the dead, and life in the world to come. This implies that the Holy Spirit, amid the whole Trinity, pours out, into, and forth into the assembly of believers, giving them the ability to wipe away sin and move toward their eternal destiny.

All of this leaves us afloat with considerable wondering.

St. John Paul II, in his encyclical *Dominum et Vivificantem*, zeroes in on what we might call the job description or position profile of the Holy Spirit. It is a lengthy one. The following reduced version attempts to highlight the major jobs entrusted to the Spirit.

The Holy Spirit:

1. Guarantees vitality and is the source of unity among believers;

2. Provides "truth and saving grace" and compels the church to do God's will;

3. Acts as second "counselor" (Christ having been the first), teaching and reminding us of God's revelation;

4. Helps the church understand Truth more fully and equips us to spread it;

5. Is, at essence, "Love-Gift," "Person-Love," "Person-Gift";

6. Communicates God's self to humans with a special interest in the poor, the suffering, and all who have open hearts;

7. Sparks holy rejoicing;

8. Sanctifies us, rooting us in the redemption and drawing us to God's kingdom;

9. Bestows "both hierarchical and charismatic gifts";

10. Clarifies what is righteous, what is sinful, what needs repentance, and invites us to conversion and forgiveness;

11. Connects God's depths and ours, gifting us with our own "secret sanctuary" of conscience and inciting us to friendship with God;

12. Transforms suffering into salvific love and self-offering;

13. Acts outside as well as inside the visible church as the impulse to truth and beauty and goodness;

14. Takes on the tug-of-war between spirit and flesh and is the champion opposing "the culture of death";

15. Builds us into temple of God and divinizes us;

16. Empowers the Eucharist and breathes our prayer.

Being godly people means that we are supposed to be Christlike, yes, but also Spiritlike. We inherit a job description that we embrace more fully as we grow in our grasp of the Spirit's mission. We are the Trinity's family, and we, who live a life in the Spirit, have been handed a legacy.

So, as spirited believers, we have to continue the family business.

We are sanctified in order to be seriously, vigorously, loving and peaceful people who are bursting with joy. We beautify the world by our faith, our prayer, our work, and our play.

≋ PRAYER

Spirit of life and love, give me that fullness of person, that willingness of gift, that will help me be the best version of myself. For my sake, for the world's sake, for God's sake.

≋ FOR REFLECTION

- One of the things fervent disciples discover is that we can't do it all. Some focus on peacemaking and social justice, some on charitable outreach, some on pro-life efforts, some on direct service to the poor, some on catechesis, some on a ministry of intercessory prayer, and so on and so on. Are there some "jobs" of the Spirit I am being nudged to take on?

- What can I do to be both passionate about my faith and better at holy rejoicing?

43 | SOUR WINE

≋ READ JOHN 19:16–42

A jar full of sour wine was standing there. So they put a sponge full of wine on a branch of hyssop and held it to his mouth. When Jesus had received the wine, he said, "It is finished." Then he bowed his head and gave up his spirit. JOHN 19:29–30

Where was the Holy Spirit on Good Friday? Comforter, Teacher, Advocate—all of these are titles and descriptions of the Spirit given by the church and elaborated on by Christian thinkers from Charles Spurgeon to John Paul II and beyond over a stretch of two and more centuries.

With all the darkness and bleakness of Good Friday, therefore, we may easily wonder where the comfort went, what got taught, and who experienced advocacy.

Among the Last Words of Jesus we find something.

St. Stephen, protomartyr and one of the first deacons of the church, echoed the Lord's "Into your hands..." When an ordinary human commends his or her spirit, as in Psalm 31 (the original source for both Jesus and Stephen), he or she certainly does not equate his or her own spirit with God's spirit. Yet our understanding of baptism and God's in-dwelling gives us pause.

If we believe that the Holy Spirit is "Lord and giver of life," as we say in the Creed, then we would have to say that our living spirit, our life-force, our human energy, partakes of the life of the Holy Spirit. We are spirited people. We have verve, zeal, love. We grow in wisdom, and we console and care for others. All of these are qualities of the Holy Spirit as well as of vibrant human beings.

If we believe, as St. John Paul II has said, that the Holy Spirit *is* personal love, then we can also say that any love in us that is genuine, lasting, and other-centered is a presence of the Holy Spirit.

Jesus, in his humanity, had all the qualities of life-giving passion and selfless love that we associate with the Holy Spirit.

We also note that the phrase "gave up his spirit" has been variously translated as delivered it, gave up the ghost, or breathed his last. When the lung capacity of the living Jesus gives out, a new creative force is breathed out—and it is, for people of faith, not a last gasp but a mighty wind. Thus, artistic crucifixes have been made to show Christ with one hand still nailed to a crossbeam but the other hand extended out and freeing a dove. They depict this mystery. The man Jesus bleeds to death and suffocates. "It is finished." And then it is truly started. The God-man sets loose the Creator Spirit to undertake a new covenant.

The blood and water flowing from the pierced side signal something both baptismal and Eucharistic. On Good Friday, this work of the Spirit is discreet. The energy is undercurrent, inhalation and exhalation, hovering over—and invisible.

Invisibility, though, is by no means absence. It sometimes means that the earth is about to quake and that everything is somehow on the verge of changing.

≋ PRAYER

Sometimes, Lord Christ, I shy away from the gory details of your death on the cross. Yet I know it is saving. Help me to grasp why an infinite, eternal, omnipotent God would give up his life-spirit for the motley crew we are.

≋ FOR REFLECTION

- On Passion Sunday and Good Friday we read the passion narrative. Even though it becomes familiar with time, what in it has struck me most powerfully in recent rereadings or rehearings?

- Have I ever attended a Passion play or a Tenebrae service? If so, what in it brought the reality of Christ's death home to me?

44 | ONE GOD, THREE NAMES

≋ READ MATTHEW 28:16–20

> And Jesus came and said to them, "All authority in heaven and on
> earth has been given to me. Go therefore and make disciples of all
> nations, baptizing them in the name of the Father and of the Son and
> of the Holy Spirit, and teaching them to obey everything that I have
> commanded you. And remember, I am with you always, to the end of
> the age." MATTHEW 28:18–20

The history of the church tells us that the followers of Christ grappled with the mystery of the Trinity, one God in three persons, from the earliest days. The New Testament, assembled soon enough by current standards, testifies that they were using the Trinitarian formula for baptism and greetings and farewell blessings very early on. That does not mean that they understood it.

We've heard the legendary story of the Christian scholar, St. Augustine, walking along the beach while struggling to make sense of the doctrine of the Trinity. We can imagine him muttering to himself. He comes upon a child who is scooting back and forth from the water's edge to a bucket he has on the beach. With a little scoop he is filling the bucket with water and likely dripping quite a bit of the sea as he rushes up the sand. The scholar asks what he is doing, and he replies that he is trying to get the sea in his bucket. Of course, the man laughs a patronizing adult laugh. You know, the kid is cute. He tells the boy that he can never put a whole ocean in a bucket. The child then turns to him and says, "And you cannot get everything about God in a human mind, either." The scholar is chastened.

That has not deterred us, however, from trying to figure out how we are a monotheistic religion and a Trinitarian one at the same time. We recite the formulas in our Sign of the Cross, in the Glorias and the Glory Bes at the end of prayers, in the Creed, and in numerous other prayers in the Eucharistic liturgy, in the celebration of sacraments, in blessings, and in all sorts of rituals and devotions.

As has been said, the way we pray is the way we believe (*lex orandi, lex credendi*). And we are quite sure that the early church spoke of the Three-in-One before recording all the gospels and epistles. That being said, we still had councils issuing decrees for centuries to clarify what we are saying and what we are not saying when we invoke Father, Son, and Spirit.

The Anglican mystic, Evelyn Underhill, has offered us some insights into how to think about the Trinity and the whole mystery of God. She says, "As Einstein conceives of space curved round the sun, we, borrowing his symbolism for a moment, may perhaps think of the world of Spirit as curved round the human soul; shaped to our finite understanding, and therefore presenting to us innumerable angles of approach. This means that God can and must be sought only within and through our human experience" (Underhill, 3). So it ought not to be shocking that we draw three circles that look like intersecting mathematic sets, or set up a triangle, or display a shamrock, or talk about the egg (shell, white, yolk) when we try to make sense of the Trinity.

St. Augustine talked about the human mind in Trinitarian terms. We hold within our minds a presence of things past, a presence of things present, and a presence of things future simultaneously in our memories, in our attentions, and in our imaginations and foresight. The problem with any of these images, of course, is that geometric figures, three-leaf clovers, eggs, and human psyches are not persons.

Underhill gives us another handy triad for thinking about the Trinity: the cosmic, the personal, the dynamic (Underhill, 10-11).

In the end, though, we cannot quite wrap our minds around the Trinity. That doesn't hold us back, however, from invoking whichever one of the persons resonates with our heart's stirring or raising our hearts and minds to all three persons simultaneously. Without seeing we believe. And so we go on proclaiming and baptizing in God's threefold name. We trust that this God is with us, always and everywhere, in fullness—even while we tap our human experiences and imagery to speak of, to, and about the God who remains Mystery.

As morning breaks, as the day goes on, and as night winds down to still, dark hours, I believe you are with me and with us. We catch glimpses and clues of you all over. Help me be aware of your gigantic reality. Help me sense your brotherly company. Help me trust that you are within me, pressing me on and blessing both my activity and rest—always.

≡ FOR REFLECTION

- Does the story of the child with the bucket settle some of my perplexity?

- Do Evelyn Underhill's insights regarding the Trinity make sense to me?

- When I try to picture God, how do I imagine the three persons individually? How do I imagine the three simultaneously? Do I have any favorite visual images of the Trinity?

45 | ACTS OF APOSTLES, ACTS OF THE SPIRIT

⟹ READ ACTS 2

Peter said to them, "Repent, and be baptized every one of you in the name of Jesus Christ so that your sins may be forgiven; and you will receive the gift of the Holy Spirit." ACTS 2:38

When it comes to the Acts of the Apostles, Father Hugo Estrada says that the real protagonist of the book is not any of the apostles but, instead, the Holy Spirit. For Estrada this New Testament book might rightly be called the Acts of the Holy Spirit.

The apostles, before the crucifixion and resurrection of Christ, had already had experiences of mission and ministry as they launched out two by two. They had their great commission both in Jesus' Last Supper discourse and at the Ascension. Yet we understand that they were fearful and that they clustered together until Pentecost. There were no clear marching orders, timetables, measurable outcomes, systems for reporting progress on goals, strategies for relating to synagogue and temple and Jewish leaders, or specifics as to what and how much of the Good News ought to be shared and with whom.

There was no business plan and an iffy corporate board. Aside from that, their lives were in danger.

All they knew to do was gather and pray.

What happens after the mighty wind and the tongues of fire, though, is a direct outcome of the coming of the Holy Spirit. The freedom to proclaim the gospel in the name of Jesus to many peoples in many tongues, the conversions of Ethiopians and Greeks and Maltese and Romans, the movement all over Asia Minor and into Europe accelerated with unearthly rapidity. Deacons were invented and a council held. Headquarters moved from Jerusalem to Rome. Unfathomable resources of mind and heart, energy and commitment came from fishermen, tentmakers, seamstresses, merchants, the poor, the wealthy, and especially one firebrand of a reformed persecutor.

They weren't quite sure themselves how it all happened. In another vein, Paul says something applicable here: "The Holy Spirit was right in saying to your ancestors through the prophet Isaiah, '…You will indeed listen, but never understand, you will indeed look but never perceive" (Acts 28:25–26). Over it all, beneath it all, around it all, the Spirit was working in ways that surpassed all comprehending. And the people acting at the Spirit's behest knew their strength and assurance was clearly not their own. There was a hidden hero who kept boosting and bolstering them.

≋ PRAYER

Give me something of that apostolic zeal, O Spirit, as I proceed through my days. And never let anything cause me to be afraid.

≋ FOR REFLECTION

- We are told that by virtue of baptism we are all called to mission. How do I participate in the missionary work of the church? Do I remember to invite the Spirit to be part of the conversation when someone asks me about my beliefs?

- Despite scandals and persecutions, people continue to join the church. Where do I find church growth most vibrant? Why do I think that is so? On the other hand, how do I account for the fact that so many American youth and young adults count themselves among the "nones," meaning that they have no religious affiliation and no particular faith? Is there something I can do to address that, even on a small scale?

➡ **READ ACTS 5:12–42**

> *But Peter and the apostles answered, "We must obey God rather than*
> *any human authority. The God of our ancestors raised up Jesus, whom*
> *you had killed by hanging him on a tree. God exalted him at his right*
> *hand as Leader and Savior... And we are witnesses to these things,*
> *and so is the Holy Spirit whom God has given to those who obey him."*
>
> ACTS 5:29–32

The Holy Spirit can be blamed for many things—and sometimes for the wackiest ideas. We find, though, that sometimes the revolutionary and unthinkable is exactly what the Spirit wants. The Biblical renewal given a jump start by Pope Pius XII; the Second Vatican Council; the liturgical renewal; the charismatic renewal; the election of popes from outside Italy—John Paul II, Benedict XVI, and Francis; the explosion of lay ministries welcomed and endorsed by the church; religious congregations' establishment of lay associates; an array of styles of spirituality and new devotions: all of these are examples. Whether we're thinking of blessed persons and devotions or actions dedicated to prayer and service, we find that the Spirit does mighty works.

Discernment is always a delicate thing. Methodologies differ considerably. After prayer and discussion, the apostles drew lots to determine which of two men should replace Judas and fill out the band of Twelve. The Council of Jerusalem entailed listening to opposing viewpoints and spending time in prayer before the church decided what to expect of Gentile converts. Anyone who wants to launch a new prayer form, a new ministry, a new mission, or a new community has to submit it to some sort of test.

Sometimes it's a matter of long experimentation, close examination, and final endorsement by religious authority. Sometimes it's a matter of agreeing that it sounds good enough and can just be floated out for a while. When it seems to be taking hold, some structure is added and hierarchical guidance is appointed. Sometimes it's a matter of study and position papers that propose that an ancient tradition ought to be revived. Examples of such processes may be found in the history of the mendicant orders (Franciscan and Dominican), the Catholic charismatic renewal, and the restoration of the permanent diaconate.

The point about any claim that something is Spirit-moved, Spirit-directed, Spirit-driven, is that someone beyond the person or small group of persons advocating it has to be involved in evaluation. Is it consistent with the mind of Christ as understood by the church? Is it wholesome, even if it seems a bit extreme (Franciscan poverty, speaking in tongues and slayings in the Spirit, allowing electricians with wives to be ordained deacons)? Does it promise to build up the body of Christ?

Gamaliel introduced to the council of Jewish elders an idea that sometimes has been used with movements that raise doubts. When Peter and the others continued to preach over the objections of the Jewish elders, Peter insisted that they were acting on orders from God. Gamaliel objected when some of the elders wanted to crush the apostles' proselytizing. He cited the number of Messianic movements that had sprung up and frittered out. The approach Gamaliel recommended was that the elders "keep away from these men and let them alone; because if this plan or this undertaking is of human origin, it will fail; but if it is of God, you will not be able to overthrow it—in that case you may even be found fighting against God."

Sometimes those who teach and lead in the church use what has been termed the Gamaliel Principle. For a while, they let be and watch. Eventually it becomes clear that what lasts must be of God: an apparition that helps convert souls; the Divine Mercy devotion; the spirituality of a woman who co-founds the Catholic Worker; the influence of a Capuchin porter in Detroit acclaimed as a miracle worker; the Communion and Liberation movement.

The Spirit knows. The church guides. A good thing, initiative, or reform, cannot be overthrown.

⋙ PRAYER

From time to time, Lord, I find devotions and mystical claims silly or scary. Give me the wisdom to wait for a weigh-in from those who understand from inside out. And keep me open to those things that waft fresh air into your house, our house.

⋙ FOR REFLECTION

- Can I name some visions, movements, or saintly people in the history of the church who were at first mistrusted? What changed our perception of them?

- In my own life, am I willing to submit my wilder ideas or personal projects to confessors, spiritual directors, trusted theologians, even bishops? Have I ever had occasion to do so? If so, how did that turn out?

47 | SEVEN FOR SERVICE

≋ READ ACTS 6

"Therefore, friends, select from among yourselves seven men of good standing, full of the Spirit and of wisdom, whom we may appoint to this task while we, for our part, will devote ourselves to prayer and to serving the word." ACTS 6:3-4

Stories about deacons don't always end in stoning to death or, as one did in recent years, in a bicycle accident initiated by a hummingbird.

Sometimes deacon stories are downright funny. Tamra Wilson has one entitled "Providence" in her collection *Dining with Robert Redford and Other Stories* (Little Creek Books, 2011). One of the yarn's main characters is an Episcopalian deacon, Presley Thurber, who tends to a woman who has had a squirrel fall hard on her head from a craggy old tree near the church graveyard. Thurber provides a bench for rest and an ice pack for her head and a chuckling walk-off to the church when another parishioner (a known UFO enthusiast) insists that this odd event must be a special sign.

Deacons were the first appointment the early church made in terms of personnel after Matthias joined the Twelve, with the possible exception of women designated to host house churches. There was a dispute about whether Greek-speaking widows were being shortchanged in food distribution. The disciples of Jesus expected a lack of distinctions among the faithful: "There is no longer Jew or Greek, there is no longer slave or free, there is no longer male and female; for all of you are one in Christ Jesus" (Galatians 3:28). On the way to implementing that belief, the apostles knew they needed to delegate responsibility so that they did not have to spend time overseeing table service and arbitrating squabbles.

The first group, men of faith and considerable virtue, were seven. St. Stephen, the first martyr, was among them.

In mission lands today and in remote areas served by Catholic Extension Society, it isn't unusual to find deacons leading church communities that are served periodically by itinerant priests. Deacons in the United States baptize, perform wedding ceremonies, catechize, assist at Eucharistic liturgies, preach, take communion to the sick, and sometimes lead parish and diocesan offices.

The restoration of the permanent diaconate since the 1970s has drawn policemen and lawyers, grocers and physicians, mechanics and professors, insurance agents and dentists to this ordained service. Men who are married, single, or widowers have been called. (In another humorous vein, it has been found that one parish in the South designates a local butcher who is also a deacon to preside over the blessing of the animals on the feast of St. Francis of Assisi.)

The Spirit initiates the desire for the diaconate, but intensive instruction, supervision, and immersion in prayer all take place for a number of years before a bishop, upon the advice of evaluators, confirms the call and qualifies the deacon through the sacrament of holy orders.

The point of the diaconate is always service, and indeed that is what the Greek word *diakonia* means. It's the ministry of the church, an outreach of the Spirit of love.

Presumably, those who are ordained have such a balanced, adaptable spirit that they can respond positively to anything from excruciating defense of the faith to ministering in zany situations with yackety-yacking parishioners in a churchyard. Deacons have to be full of solemnity as well as humor as the need arises.

Spirit, instill in me a respect for clergy and an understanding that you equip and qualify those you call. Help me to understand that, in your name, we become more than just ourselves. Let me see how you strengthen us for your service by the variety of charisms you pour out.

≡ **FOR REFLECTION**

- Again, with the selection of deacons, discernment enters in. How do I see it working?

- Why is it significant that the diaconate is particularly egalitarian (at least among baptized males)—in its membership as well as its outreach?

- The question of a diaconate for women has been raised for some time and is officially under study. What have I learned about the history of the diaconate amid the press this has been given?

48 | WHAT HOLY SPIRIT?

READ ACTS 19:1-7

[Paul] said to them, "Did you receive the Holy Spirit when you became believers?" They replied, "No, we have not even heard that there is a Holy Spirit." ACTS 19:2

So, did you receive the Spirit when you were baptized? How were you baptized?

Among Christians, there are differences of opinion about who should be baptized and at what age. When it comes to youth and adults, must baptism always be preceded by a rigorous RCIA process? Should every roadway be made straight before baptism? Must one remain a long-term catechumen if there are some crooked lines in one's living arrangements and marital status? And what do we do in polygamous tribal areas? Which of the wives gets to stay if a husband desires to convert, and what happens to the children? Is infant baptism really the best idea, especially if it's Grandma who is pushing it and not Mom and Dad? Is immersion in water preferable to pouring?

We hear that in the early days, an Ethiopian eunuch was baptized on the spot by Philip after a bit of instruction in how to interpret Scripture. When the prayerful, hospitable Lydia was baptized by Paul, her whole household converted. In both cases, the baptisms seem to have been in river water. And it does sound as though desire carried more weight than long sessions of instruction. Infant baptism seems implicit when we begin talking about whole households, though it isn't certain when the practice actually began. These baptisms presume that the Holy Spirit is activated at baptism but has a lot of work to do to get the message of Christ and the obligations of discipleship internalized.

So our baptism is an unrepeatable event with fascinating outcomes, but it is also a process. Our reception of the Holy Spirit seems especially so. For some, the sacrament of confirmation is a clinching moment. For others, however, even that seems more like a time for a family get-together than a profound encounter with God. Something more is needed.

For some of us, it is a retreat at which we become more aware of the presence of the Spirit. For some it is involvement in a charismatic prayer group. For others, a Cursillo weekend or an opportunity to make the Spiritual Exercises of St. Ignatius Loyola ignites us. For still others, it is a ministerial experience that has built into it times for reflection and faith sharing. Whatever the way in religious settings, we find ourselves more attuned to the Holy Spirit and more ready to perceive the lasting impact of our confirmation. We can be moved by hymns or any beautiful thing that awakens us to the Holy Spirit.

A tangled problem unravels, a blessed peace descends, and we know that Someone else has been pulling the strings. We may have heard of the Holy Spirit, but the chances are very good that there are special moments when we realize that the Spirit is a living and present person.

Where the going gets tough is seeing and sensing the Holy Spirit everywhere, involved in everything. Where and how does the Spirit reside in the world's sin and the tragedies endlessly reported on Fox and CNN? How is the Spirit hovering over Myrtle Beach's Crown Reef Hotel, purple lit on its southwest side by night, as bikers roar along Ocean Boulevard? Families on a short autumn vacation mix with corporate types who have prospered by exporting jobs to countries with no minimum wage laws constraining their activities.

In such a place, we have to believe that the Spirit is available to all. The Spirit is in the beat of tides lapping over rosary-sayers as well as women who spend exorbitant amounts at nearby outlets. On a global scale, we profess that the Spirit must be and should be where hundreds and thousands die of muddy water, ruined food, and undelivered medical supplies.

Learning where the Spirit is when thrill-seekers go aloft in hot air balloons over an American beach resort takes the gift of understanding. Where that Spirit is in a pot-bellied, pock-marked motherless child shown in a mission magazine requires understanding too. We want to know, and we struggle to say, how the Holy Spirit surrounds us at our desks while a passenger plane drops off the radar screen somewhere in Mongolia.

Wearing a small dove lapel pin does not suffice to make us devotees. The process of receiving the Spirit requires opening again and again to the mysteries, the contraries and contradictions, the vagaries of life, its auto-wrecked little animals, its indefatigable monarch butterflies, its mackerel catch, and its shark bite.

Even if we have heard of the Holy Spirit, we continue to try to figure out how the Spirit works. For those who haven't heard at all, it's a tall order for us to begin, little by little, to explain.

⇒ PRAYER

Spirit of the living God, I give thanks that I have heard of you—for years, in fact. Let me know more of your works, and make me part of them so that I may live in you.

⇒ FOR REFLECTION

- What experiences or episodes have made the Holy Spirit more real to me?

- How would I begin to explain the Spirit to one who has never heard of the Holy Spirit?

- Do I have any pet theories or wise sayings that help me understand situations that make no sense to me?

49 | KNOWING WHAT WE DO NOT KNOW

➔ READ 1 CORINTHIANS 2:1–11

The Spirit searches everything, even the depths of God.

1 CORINTHIANS 2:10B

Sometimes we know things that we didn't know we knew. It's not so much an answer to a riddle or a word for a crossword puzzle or a question on *Jeopardy*. It's more an intuition as to what is troubling someone or what he or she might truly need or when it's just the right time to do or say something. On a deeper level, Wordsworth remarked poetically that we receive "intimations of immortality" by being attentive.

Attentiveness is the core trait of the contemplative. It is attunement to both the surfaces of things, in all their details, and the realities below or beyond the surfaces. The reality below and beyond is what St. Paul alludes to here.

There are tectonic shifts that precede earthquakes, bubbles of lava that seep up before huge eruptions, chunks of ice falling off bergs and recessions of permafrost that forewarn of sea level rise. Similarly, the soul is tilled for the seeds of evangelization by a restlessness of spirit, a sense that there is a hole in one's heart or soul, a desire for more, a yearning for meaning. We get the feeling that we almost know something, but we are not sure what it is. It is like the feeling that someone is in a room when we cannot see a form or pick up a scent.

The fertilization of that tilled field of our soul may happen by way of an out-of-the-blue question asked by a friend or neighbor. One feels oddly quizzical and then may find an unbidden happiness, even giddiness, overtaking one's bones. It's almost as if we're on the verge of winning the lottery or discovering a new continent or a new planet. We somehow just know something is going on, something is about to be revealed.

St. Paul speaks about the small steps sometimes required when one is dealing with potential converts. Once there is a glad curiosity about the good news of Christ, it may take some spoon-feeding. The gospel and the subtleties of Christian faith may have to be delivered via Gerber baby food and warm formula before the person is up to arugula and pine nuts in the salad, and filet mignon, twice-baked potatoes, and asparagus as entrée. There are mysteries to be unfolded: the Paschal Mystery, the implications of the New Testament and the linkages with the Old, the celebration of liturgy, moral teaching, liberation from sin, the Trinity, the communion of saints, the promise of eternity, to name a few.

What Paul suggests is that the Holy Spirit, who is so real as to be palpably felt at times, is in the process of unveiling the God who has been by and large hidden in the heart of the person who is not yet even a catechumen. The Spirit is also unveiling human destiny, and there is something in us that just knows there is so much more to know—about divinity and humanity.

The Corinthians may have had intimations in terms of a desire for more, a search for meaning, an availability to grace just because they had been exposed to the idea of gods and the beauty of visual art and architecture. The Spirit, Paul suggests, works there because the Spirit knows not only us and our deepest longings but also the depths of God.

Sometimes, when we are clattering around the kitchen at midnight looking for potato chips and seltzer water or God knows what, we might wonder whether we are actually itching for something much more substantial, something that feeds our soul. The Spirit will know us and will know how to fill us. If we attend to our own depths, we will realize this.

And so, good God, I ask: What more do you want me to know? How deep does your Spirit want me to go?

≡ **FOR REFLECTION**

- As I think back on my journey in faith, what were some moments when I had inklings about something that became much clearer as I learned and lived the faith?

- Catechesis and Christian formation are the terms we use for instruction in the faith. What kinds of things are appropriate for us when we are at the beginner level? What things when we are newly initiated? What kinds of things when we are more mature?

- At this stage in my life, what spiritual resources are most helpful to me? What challenges me now to grow?

50 | THE WORLDLY SPIRIT

READ 1 CORINTHIANS 2:12–16

Now we have received not the spirit of the world, but the Spirit that is from God, so that we may understand the gifts bestowed on us by God.

1 CORINTHIANS 2:12

There is a difference between being appreciative of earthly blessings and being worldly. We can relish the daylong sounds of birds and the nightlong burps of frogs and hoots of owls. We can listen happily for train whistles. We can revel in the soundscapes played by the stations on cable or use our season concert tickets gladly. We can find shopping recreational and love to see what people do with their homes on HGTV. We can have enthusiasm for our favorite teams and find good company at tailgate parties. We can get a kick out of experimenting with recipes or tinkering with cars. We can bless God for education and vacations.

Worldliness goes beyond all this. It entails a preoccupation with things, particularly superficial things. Worldliness overspends, gluts, pursues, measures personal value in acquisitions and toys, achieves at all costs, and wastes hours, days, months, and years on trivia. Worldliness hoards and ignores those who lack. It cheats on God and is stingy with its parish and with charities—if it bothers with them at all. Worldliness grooms, clothes, scents, and jewels itself to death. And it collects and collects and collects.

The spirit of the world is all about over-emphasis and excess. It evaluates in terms of cost and capital gains.

The Spirit of God allows us to accept and use the gifts of this world graciously but also to find ways to give them away or, if need be, go without. The Spirit reminds us of the first and third Beatitudes pronounced by the Lord in the Sermon on the Mount. Enough is enough, the Holy Spirit says. Less is often more. Simplify.

God's Kingdom and the earth itself belong to the poor in spirit and the meek. The Paraclete, the Advocate, cautions us that abundance is by and large invisible.

⋙ PRAYER

Spirit of letting go, help me to understand better how to be in the world but not of it. I live in a consumerist culture and am in so many ways rich compared to the rest of the world. Give me the grace to appreciate what I have and what comes but also to give it over. Let me be more empty-handed and more generous every day.

⋙ FOR REFLECTION

- Who for me are the best models of simple living and poverty of spirit?

- What are the first steps I need to take to simplify my life and dispense with unnecessary goods? What discipline might I need to balance the time I spend?

51 | THE SPIRIT OF THE CITY

≋ READ 2 CORINTHIANS 3:7-18

Now the Lord is the Spirit, and where the Spirit of the Lord is,
there is freedom. 2 CORINTHIANS 3:17

In Detroit, on Woodward Avenue, at the corner of Jefferson, a muscular, graceful bronze figure holds a golden sun in his left hand and a golden trio of woman, child, and man in his right.

Behind this statue, called "The Spirit of Detroit," are these engraved words: "Now the Lord is that Spirit and where the Spirit of the Lord is, there is liberty."

Not far, just across Hart Plaza, along the bank of the deep Detroit River, facing Windsor is another statue: "The Underground Railroad." This is a massive memorial of men, women, and children, some with uplifted faces, some with raised eyes, one turned to point the way to all the people we can imagine behind him. All are African American. All are in the put-together calico dresses, flannel trousers, homespun shirts, rough jackets, and knit shawls of the nineteenth-century slave era. Detroit was free, but Windsor, Canada, was safer. No one there would send an escaped slave back to someone who owned a plantation. Detroit offered a conduit but not safe haven once the Fugitive Slave Act was in force.

There's a lot to be said, though, for Detroit and for Michigan. It was a religious culture at its founding. Its history includes a broad tolerance of faith traditions, a resounding no to the institution of slavery, prohibition of capital punishment from its first law-making, efforts to empower and celebrate the gifts of minorities, and welcome to enclaves of immigrants.

On the other hand, Detroit is in some ways held captive by the auto industry, which effectively dismantled public transportation decades back to promote vehicles that would rob their citizens' breath. Michigan still is building gargantuan homes, excessive malls, and inevitable ranks of storage buildings on what were once wildflowered prairies and wetlands.

All that having been said, Detroit, in its statue form, invites the citizen and visitor to liberty. Its very form is muscular yet flowing, sitting steady and lotus-like while reaching out and up—to the heavens and to terra firma.

Liberty is found where people can flourish and be family, where they can look to a nearby shore and breathe free. Liberty stands firm against violence and lets life be. It is the pursuit of truth, wherever that pursuit may lead, and the speaking of one's mind. It is free jazz in Hart Plaza and the Amistad docked so that people both take ease and remember pain. Liberty is a truce between police and the homeless which lets them sleep on grassy banks. Liberty is, too, a quiet vista where a lonely woman or man may recall that she or he still loves even when mutuality, reciprocity, and response have been lost.

Liberty is Catholic Mass at noon, a woman in a hijab walking by at 1:00, and a Hasid in sidecurls leading a school of boys in yarmulkes down the steps of a public building at 2:00. Liberty is water, food, air, camaraderie, and the hope that lets us be who we are and fuels our dreams.

Paul and the Corinthians never foresaw Detroit. But our faith knows that the Spirit builds cities, frees slaves, and erects monuments. Glory is meant to abound not only later but here and now.

⩸ PRAYER

Spirit of God, I know that we can't find or create heaven on earth, but there are moments when heaven seems to break through. Help me appreciate such moments and also help create them.

⩸ FOR REFLECTION

- Where have I found specific biblical signs and references in secular settings and in government structures?

- Do I sense that the Holy Spirit has been part of the making of my city, town, or rural area? Is that publicly acknowledged? If so, how or by whom?

52 | FRUITS OF THE SPIRIT

≡ **READ GALATIANS 5:13–26**

Now the works of the flesh are obvious…By contrast, the fruit of the Spirit is love, joy, peace, patience, kindness, generosity, faithfulness, gentleness, and self-control. GALATIANS 5:19, 22–23

The deplorable behaviors Paul calls the products of unfettered flesh—everything from rivalries and dissensions to drunkenness and orgies—spark the headlines of tabloids. They're the carryings-on associated with the palatial closets and billowing chambers of kings and queens, madams and matadors, pricey escorts and fraternity brothers. The varieties of misconduct are pedestal-toppling, the risky hire-wire walks of high society or professional hierarchs gone low-life.

Benedictine Scripture scholar Eugene Hensell speaks of how the biblical prophets again and again had to rail against an onslaught of "royal consciousness" afflicting the people of Israel. He speaks about their potential for succumbing to a sense of privilege and entitlement. When riches, flamboyance, military muscle, and expectations of adulation became the character and stamp of the descendants of David, the covenant was besmirched. The people's reliance on God frittered away amid their distractions. The prophets repeatedly denounced the glitter that overlaid the Decalogue with dust and tipped the scales against the poor, the ill, the voiceless, and the landless.

Paul realized that the same corruptibility can worm its way into the church. It happens when the born-again lose their fervor and revert to business as usual while they remain only nominally or half-heartedly in Christ.

Today, believers may fall for the cult of the athlete, the rock star, the actor, the casino builder, the billionaire geek, or whoever happens to be the latest newsmaker of the day. Ask a group of seven- or eight-year-olds what they'd like to be when they grow up, and there will surely be some who respond, "a celebrity!" Press a bit more, and it becomes clear that they have no idea what a celebrity does or how she or he makes a living. They merely know that some celebrities live in big posh houses, take amazing vacations, and arrive at intoxicating events in chauffeur-driven cars. They elicit shouts and cheers and applause and camera flashes and are gorgeously coiffed and clothed and manicured.

Celebrity consciousness displaces attention from canonizations of people like John Paul II and Teresa of Kolkata. Celebrity consciousness blows off enrollment in the St. Vincent de Paul Society, Pax Christi, the Catholic Worker, the Christian Appalachian Project, or participation in rallies for life. Why? Perhaps because the life of virtue, dedication to prayer, and loving-kindness can seem insufferably dull to a hyper-stimulated world.

Paul's recitation of the fruits of the Spirit isn't a headline maker. It is, however, a life maker, a family sustainer, a community enhancer, a Kingdom builder. These virtues, these fruits, are found not in royal consciousness or celebrity stalking but in Christ.

The Spirit overtops and stops the crazed nightlife, the divorce-go-round, the klieg lights, and the rise and fall of the very forgettable superstar.

The Spirit *is* love and *in* us. When we are in God, we are white-hot. That is all the status anyone requires.

⇒ PRAYER

Spirit, forgive me for the times I made a bigger deal of a superstar or a Pulitzer Prize winner than I did of you. Forget the times I wasted on passing fancies and glitter. Make me a spender of constructive, beneficent time.

⇒ FOR REFLECTION

- What are the distractions that pull me away from deeper, kinder things? What do I have to do to redirect my attention?

- When I waste time, what excuses do I give myself—my age, my health, my need for relaxation, my mental fatigue, my physical fatigue, what? Are my excuses really valid?

- Am I willing to search the spirit in me to discover the sins the Confiteor refers to in terms of things we do and things we fail to do?

53 | IN OUR HEARTS

READ EPHESIANS 3:14-21

I pray that, according to the riches of his glory, he may grant that you may be strengthened in your inner being with power through his Spirit.

EPHESIANS 3:16

There is such a thing as heart knowledge, and we are supposed to have a cornucopia of it. The source of its spillway of fruits is love. And it is Christ's love that we understand as having all "breadth and length and height and depth" of love that is poured out for and fed into us.

Thus, we know that there is a God, that Christ is really present in the Eucharist, that the Holy Spirit is vigorously alive, that the church embraces saints and sinners, that we are called to do good and avoid evil, that we are meant for love, and that our lives matter.

We also know, however, that our hearts aren't always quite right. We have our moments of brilliance and compassion and blessed drive to achieve. That's for sure. But we also realize—sometimes during, sometimes after—that our heart's desires and our heart's leanings are not, and have not always been, right. We are capable of misjudging situations or choosing the worst possible timing.

We can also con ourselves into thinking that our most self-serving or even salacious yearnings are what God thinks we deserve. In such cases, we convince ourselves that our hearts are right and all the good counsel in the world is dead wrong. We're enlightened and ahead of our times, we imagine.

Father Andrew Apostoli has observed that the danger of applying misguided heart knowledge to our lives and personal dilemmas is that we end up rejecting God-ordained guidance. When we reject the collective wisdom of the successors of the apostles and the saints in Christ's church, we reject the Holy Spirit. We believe that we hold an "interior enlightenment of the Holy Spirit," Apostoli says, but mistakenly apply it. Such misguided apprehension of what is leading us leads "people to assume they have that 'inner light' and the principle of personal interpretation is the norm of truth" (Apostoli, 42).

So then what? Having a heart's communication that something is "right for me" does not necessarily ring true, and we have to realize that. Philosophers and ethicists say that ethical action has to be assessed in terms of its ability to be applied universally. Would the world be better if everybody everywhere was determined to live by my rules and my inner lights?

The "breadth and length and height and depth" of Christ's love give us the lights to discern as long as we remain truly honest with ourselves. Heart knowledge can be so, so right, but it also has to be willing to be played out and to connect with others' lights. These others should be recognized for their gift of counsel, their Spirit-filled insight and ability to guide. If we really entrust ourselves to heart knowledge, we have to be both confident and submissive.

When Paul prays for the church at Ephesus, he knows its members are full of love. But he also knows that passionate love, even passionate love we believe we have for God, sometimes must be redirected. Saint-making tends to trim our hearts of the clutter of our own stuff.

⫸ PRAYER

Spirit of love, live in my heart. Spirit of understanding, guide me to read my own heart wisely. Spirit of counsel, teach me to listen and grow in wise directions.

⫸ FOR REFLECTION

- Devotion to the Sacred Heart of Jesus is one of the many ways that the church has developed to help us cultivate our hearts and guard our hearts and align our hearts with Christ's. Am I familiar with St. Margaret Mary Alacoque and these devotions?

- St. Ignatius Loyola taught the Jesuits to listen to the hearts of their directees. He also taught them to ask honest questions about whether something a person desired was from the Holy Spirit, from his or her own spirit, or from the evil spirit. How do I suppose one would begin to know?

54 | PRAYER IN THE SPIRIT

READ EPHESIANS 6:10–23

Pray in the Spirit at all times in every prayer and supplication.

EPHESIANS 6:18

Everywhere and at all times, gratitude is, as Brother David Steindl-Rast and others have said, at the heart of prayer. That perhaps is the best way we can understand the saying that the Spirit prays in us. After threats of hurricanes have passed and we find our trees still standing and our homes intact, the garden flowers unripped, the water uncontaminated, and the lights still on, we sigh a massive Thank You. We also rejoice in happy surprises, an unusually rapid and unqualified yes to a proposal, the unexpected visitor we've fondly hoped to see again, a bequest that falls from heaven and fills a need for our favorite charity. We find ourselves grateful for mugs of morning coffee, bowls of warm, buttery grits, and crisp strips of bacon. We've been spared.

Yet we grieve too as we get weighted down by news of volcanic eruptions and earthquakes, wildfires blasting homes away, and murders perpetrated by racists and terrorists who target unsuspecting innocents. We mourn the adolescent suicide and the family wiped out by a drunk driver. We weep within for those who live in waist-deep mud around tin shelters that are emptied of everything. We cannot comprehend that there are children drying to bones for lack of food and water. Brigades of volunteers from the Red Cross and the armed services barely seem to touch extensive devastation, and too many murders, rapes, and thefts go unsolved. We have far too many causes needing supplication. Add to that familial, workplace, and political madness, and we have an endless string for our intercessory prayer.

Paul knew that we praise, thank, beg forgiveness, and raise our voices on behalf of others. We also go back to our routines, to our morning offerings, to our tiny reasons for joy and gladness, knowing all the while that our world is frayed and has not been and will not be one without miracles. Paul knew that he needed, and we desperately need, the leverage of prayer.

⇒ PRAYER

God of all, you are larger than our lives. Widen our view and expand our possibilities—way beyond our small and all too local gratitude. In-spirit us for our whole global community.

⇒ FOR REFLECTION

- How world-conscious is my prayer? That is to say, how big is my heart?

55 | BUBBLY CHRISTIANITY

⇒ **READ 1 THESSALONIANS 5**

Rejoice always, pray without ceasing, give thanks in all circumstances; for this is the will of God in Christ Jesus for you. Do not quench the Spirit. 1 THESSALONIANS 5:16–19

Cardinal Avery Dulles, so well-known for his *Models of the Church*, has observed that Christ has always been regarded as the head but that the Holy Spirit ought to be thought of as the heart and soul of the church (Dulles, 57).

If there is a good illustration of the affective-spiritual aspect of the church anywhere, it's in these verses near the end of 1 Thessalonians. The picture of the church as a community of disciples that Paul proposes is that of a happy, prayerful, grateful group. One can imagine a cadre of close friends bonded in fellowship and attentive to whatever new and challenging thing the Spirit brings. They are to expect some surprises, some holy effervescence from the Holy Spirit, and they are not shy about expressing excitement.

When we are mindful of this injunction on the early followers of Christ to be full of rejoicing, we have to recall the double-sidedness of this. On the one hand, they were sure they were on a happy journey, heaven-bound. On the other hand, they were faced with massive misunderstanding and rejection at best—and torture and martyrdom at worst. It's somehow hard to picture perpetual good humor under such circumstances.

But that is what Paul calls for: Rejoice! Be joyful! Pay attention to all your blessings! Keep saying Thank You!

It's often said that happy believers and cheerful sufferers are the best advertisement for Christianity. If we've got the Spirit, it would seem that we ought to be irrepressible, no matter what. Heart and soul!

Put that joyful Spirit, O Lord, right on my face—right where I need it!

- We don't often think of Christianity in terms of comedy, but can laughter be a sign of the presence of the Holy Spirit? Are there times I have seen evidence of that—in others, in certain situations, or in me?

- Father James Martin, SJ, has written a whole book on joy and humor entitled *Between Heaven and Mirth*. Hilarity is not joy, but his study does demonstrate that a capacity for being fun-loving is and can be quite saintly. Am I willing to give it a try?

⇒ **READ TITUS 3:1-8**

He saved us, not because of any works of righteousness that we had done, but according to his mercy, through the water of rebirth and renewal by the Holy Spirit. TITUS 3:5

Often we give only grudgingly. We will do kindly deeds or go extra miles or surrender our convenience, but only so far. We will manage somehow to protect our time and to hold our privacy in reserve.

We go only so far in faith. and in changes of mind too. We believe but back ourselves up with security systems, Plan B, some safe recourse. We listen with seeming openness but hold onto our own thoughts. Or we appear to bare our souls but hold some secrets that are our very selves in reserve. We let ourselves be challenged, and we'll venture to take new steps, but we're sure the soles of our shoes are reinforced and sufficiently rubberized that we don't squeak.

Sometimes, though, something comes. An overwhelming human need, a demand upon our love, a revelation that crashes upon us with its irrefutable and irresistible truth, or a call to let go: whatever it is, we know that we can do nothing but respond and do what must be done or believe what must be believed.

Paul, writing to Titus in Crete, was aware that some of the believers had been stifled souls—stifled by bad habits and by their secrets. He knew that they would need to ungrip their fists, let their tense shoulders relax, and gently exhale their choke-held breath. He was confident that this loosening would not weaken their commitment to Christ but would, instead, loosen the hold of old ways. As he attests to Titus, "We ourselves were once foolish, disobedient, led astray, slaves to various passions and pleasures, passing our days in malice and envy, despicable, hating one another." The Savior had made the difference.

The old ways were what kept some of the giving only grudging and some of the kindly deeds and surrender bland. The bad habits made trust uneasy. Paul's pep talk emphasizes the virtues Titus should himself exemplify as well as teach. He would un-stifle souls by offering the model and means of living a life in Christ. That's what Paul said ought to be expected of a rebirth.

In some ways, Spirit, I think of myself as a long-time Christian. Remind me that we are always needful of rebirth and renewal in some crevices of our being. Help me scrape off the barnacles of the past that still cling to my spirit.

≈ **FOR REFLECTION**

- Some evangelization entails inculturation—that is, adopting and adapting elements of a particular culture to worship and the practices of faith. We might think of the Day of the Dead customs of Mexicans around All Souls Day or the Christmas trees introduced by the Christians of Germany. At times, though, those who are brought into the community of faith have to abandon some familiar customs. What are some elements of our own American culture that do not square with our commitment to Christ? What does it take to let go of these practices as we become more imbued with the Spirit?

57 | WISDOM FROM ABOVE

⮚ **READ JAMES 3:13-18**

But the wisdom from above is first pure, then peaceable, gentle, willing to yield, full of mercy and good fruits, without a trace of partiality or hypocrisy. And a harvest of righteousness is sown in peace for those who make peace. JAMES 3:17-18

Not once does the Letter of James mention the Holy Spirit. He does talk of wisdom, generosity, and the admonition to the Lord's followers to be "doers of the word." He cautions against partiality, the sins of the tongue, conflicts among the members, and the corruptions of the rich. As is well known, he shows that faith and good works are integrally linked.

Since he introduces the image of "the Father of lights," it's possible to give some thought to what we know of light and lighthouses. The Spirit, we may recall, is with some frequency compared to light. Light in our planetary experience is a creation, the first of all creatures as Genesis 1 has it. Light comes of, in, and from the singularity with which the cosmos began. It is unaccountable unless one posits that something can come from nothing and that the nothing from which God creates allows the photons characteristic of light to come into existence.

The prismed light from lighthouses, generated by artifice, is a human invention. In the light of lighthouses, we can imagine that the divine and the human meet. The light guides and guards whatever it may, wil-ly-nilly, night after night, no matter whether anyone, no one, someone or nearly everyone is at sea or watching from the coastline. The light blares through cloudy and clear sky. The light of the lighthouse is something like the word of God, borne by the Spirit, in season and out, ever available, no matter what.

Old Presque Isle Lighthouse in Michigan has about it qualities of the Gospel according to St. Mark. The house is brief, even stubby, blunted but adequate. It's on enough of a bluff. It's visible and doesn't need great length or height. In Mark, Jesus walks. He goes into the wilderness. He's tempted. He comes back. He says, "Come." Some do. He says, "Repent." Some hear. He tells some stories. They're short. A seed gets planted. It grows, nondescript. The farmer hardly notices. But it sprouts and yields. Jesus heals. He instructs. He works with a few rustics who barely get the point. Simon Peter figures something out. The Messiah goes up to Jerusalem. He breaks bread, sweats, is taken captive, dies on a cross. A Roman centurion figures something out. Days later, some women find an empty tomb. No one knows what to say. We, the ones who come after, fill in the details. We pray the in-between. We preach the story and Word is made flesh again.

Mark is the Hemingway of the gospels. All one really needs is a clean, well-lighted place, a place for a quick meal and coffee, a place where there's someone to talk to for a few minutes. God knows. We need a light that stays on late—or always.

The New Presque Isle Lighthouse and the lighthouse at Sturgeon Pointe are Matthew and Luke. They're derivative and original. They do what Mark does, but there's a Sermon on the Mount or a Sermon on the Plain. There are Jewish forebears, Jewish roots, patriarchs and prophets filtered through, or there are angels, shepherds, women, Gentiles, a good Samaritan. The light splays from higher up. But there's the same whitewashed brick, the same bulbous peak and point to the lighthouse tower, the same spiral stairs and windowed landings on the way up. The signal flashes on the same principle of surprisingly low wattage and perfectly calculated prisms. The light flashes to all eyes that see on a Lake Huron night.

The lighthouse at Tawas is something like 69 feet high, lofting into clear sky. There are few bushes or trees at its base, so it reaches exultantly. It is the Gospel according to St. John. Jesus is water, bread, light, and way. He is blue sky, flecks of cloud, deep breath, the lighthouse seems to say. He meets, greets, touches, loves, but always points above. He speaks, sometimes mysteriously, and heaven shines upon earth. The eye follows the lighthouse to its knob and spire and know that there is safety in the night, another light unseen by day, an in-breaking of care.

Amen, the lighthouses say. Let dark and thunder come. Let cloud enwrap. But light still is, and blue sky will be. The stretch of the heavens will be more numerous. The sun will rise and shine and warm. The reign of God overcomes.

And, in the meantime, God's Spirit reigns wherever beauty breaks. There is wisdom, generosity, and good-doing in tall towers, prismed light, spiral stairways, keepers' houses, the berries and pines that grow not far away, and the gulls and herons that swoop and veer.

⇛ PRAYER

Source of Light, Spirit of Wisdom, shine steadily on me, and let me grow in the Word through the gospels you have inspired. Let me too bear light and keep light for those who would see.

⇛ FOR REFLECTION

- The Letter of James is filled with imagery of waves at sea, flowers in fields, tame creatures, and patient farmers. Why might his letter rely on earthy comparisons for teaching?

- If you were to choose a metaphor or simile to represent likenesses and differences in the gospels, what, aside from the lighthouse, might seem to you to work?

⇒ READ 2 PETER

First of all you must understand this, that no prophecy of scripture is a matter of one's own interpretation, because no prophecy ever came by human will, but men and women moved by the Holy Spirit spoke from God. 2 PETER 1:20–21

There's something about humans that is drawn to palm readings, Tarot cards, psychic hotlines, horoscopes, and fortune-telling. We're always on the verge of news flash or breakthrough, we think, and it's surely going to be something like striking gold—or hearing the doomsday forecast just in time to get away. Good news or bad, we're always looking for a way to spin it or know the scoop before anyone else gets it. There's something about us that wants to be in when it comes to inner circles or occult knowledge.

Prophecy, though, is more about the inside story that is not exotic and, in fact, ought to be fairly transparent to us if we are in the know in a faith-filled way. Whether the topic is some hard-core truth hot off the press or end-time predictions, we seekers want reliable sources. Really. Inner circle stuff that comes from a sure-fire, time-tested inner circle. Divine revelation and its authentic interpreters offer just that.

The Second Letter of Peter grapples with three major issues:

1. What virtues support authentic knowledge of Christ?

2. How do we deal with the proliferation of false prophets and outright heresies?

3. Why has the Second Coming of Christ not happened yet?

All of these matters are interwoven.

Depending upon the translation, we read either that faith undergirds a list of Christian qualities—virtue, discernment, self-control, perseverance, piety, fraternal care, and love (NAB)—or that Christian love is the foundation on which mutual affection, godliness, endurance, self-control, knowledge, goodness, and faith rest (NRSV). Whether it's ascending or descending order, the text makes it clear that the virtues build one upon the other and that the disciple of Christ is called to live a virtuous life. A virtuous life provides the necessary support for knowledge of Christ.

When it comes to the question of prophets and prophecies, 2 Peter makes it clear that the Hebrew prophets and the teaching of Christ are the reliable sources. Those who claim new insights, contradict the foundations of faith, and lead people astray are the ones who tend to give themselves away as false prophets. Sensuality, greed, and self-seeking may be the tip-off. And somehow they seem to be the independent source of their own purported revelations. We might compare them to those in our own time who have discounted biblical testimony, time-tested doctrine and moral teaching, along with magisterial authority, because they deem it old-fashioned, out of style, rigid, and nastily judgmental.

New religions and new denominations and upside-down internal revolts in long-established churches pop up and market their wares regularly. But the faithful have been warned for nearly two thousand years that there will be voices promoting new approaches and refuting time-honored beliefs. They will be claiming justice, charity, and liberal-mindedness. They will say they have prayed and discerned. What the church has always noted, as Peter points out, is that not every spirit campaigning for a new way is the Holy Spirit. The test is whether the new idea or the proposed revision is consonant with the law, the prophets, and the teachings of Jesus—and whether the one who has generated a prophecy is the same Spirit that has taken up residence in the heart of the faithful.

The third question is the one which has apparently led, almost from the beginning of Christianity, to a proliferation of folks who want to name when the Second Coming will happen or, lacking its advent, want out. The delay in the Second Coming of Christ did indeed take the early church off guard. For a considerable time, they expected an imminent return of the Lord in glory. This gave scoffers a heyday. They discredited the Way taught by Jesus because they thought the delay rendered his Good News worthless. The response of Peter, however, puts the idea of the return in a whole new light, and it is an insight which is now well known. "With the Lord one day is like a thousand years," he says, "and a thousand years are like one day. The Lord is not slow about his promise…but is patient with you, not wanting any to perish, but all to come to repentance."

Peter takes the long view. God has God's own sense of timing and, after all, dwells outside the realm of time. Time itself is God's creation, and we know now, even more than was dreamed in the days of Peter, how old the universe, our galaxy, our solar system, and our own planet are. They are unimaginably more ancient than anyone can comprehend.

Part of this long view also supports, or at least lends credence to, some theological reflections about universal salvation. While Scripture and Tradition have always held that rational beings can permanently set themselves against God and thus be for all eternity separated from God in hell, no one has ever said definitely that anyone, other than the devil and his fallen angels, are in that condition. Hans Urs von Balthasar was among those who hoped that God's mercy might be so wide that even at the last millisecond a soul could turn to God and be saved.

Maybe that is what we are waiting for while some of our Christian comrades put up billboards and stick on bumper stickers announcing when the last day is. We may find ourselves very grateful that the Spirit hasn't prophesied a divine deadline for changes of heart and a turn God-ward.

Spirit of God, lead me to pay attention to the voices that bear your good tidings, and help me to have the humility to know when I need simply to wait. Do not let me be overtaken by spiritual and moral fraud! And have mercy on those who would mislead.

≋ **FOR REFLECTION**

- How do I deal with those who are consumed by ideas about the Rapture and fixated on what they believe are signs that the end of the world is imminent?

- What do I imagine it will be like when Christ does come? Is it possible that the Second Coming will be gradual and subtle, a non-stupendous but decisive process? If so, what might that look like?

- Are there resources that have helped me get in touch with both the expanse of time and the immensity of eternity (for example, the eleventh chapter of St. Augustine's *Confessions*)?

> *But you, beloved, must remember the predictions of the apostles...*
> *[that] "there will be scoffers, indulging their own ungodly lusts." It is*
> *these worldly people, devoid of the Spirit, who are causing divisions.*
> JUDE 17–19

Liturgy is sensuous. It uses color, music, candlelight, glinting sacred vessels, incense, bells, and recitative prayers. Masses, especially the more festal, solemn ones, fill the senses.

Art, music, drama, and poetry are sensuous too. They stir the heart and stimulate the imagination and every sensory faculty. Family albums, photos, and videos posted on social media do the same.

An example of a sensuous poem shows how this works. Betty Adcock speaks of the sensory splay of memory that comes after a death. In a little book entitled *Widow Poems* (Jacar Press, 2014), she takes her reader on a walk through an old house, pointing out a vase, a stairway, a "jigsaw quilt" in a bedroom, a hooked rug, a sofa where a baby sat, a kitchen where birthday cakes were baked, and she wonders: "Why is it then, we never took a photograph of rooms/we lived in, their tackle and trim...?" ("The Widow Tries to Say It, without Philosophy, Theology, or Grief," 8).

We get the scene vividly. The things of this world populate the widow's memory, and along with her we want to immortalize the roses, the quilt, the rug, and we want to hear forever the mewling sounds of the baby. We pick up the pangs of loss and absence. It's a little memoir of the senses.

Sensuality, the problem of those "indulging...ungodly lusts," is something quite different. Not unlike ourselves, the believers of Jude's era found themselves beset by some who proclaimed themselves definitely saved and consequently free to do all sorts of things.

We've often heard St. Augustine cited for the saying, "Love God and do as you please." It's easily misconstrued to mean that since *we're* justified *anything* is. Rightly interpreted, Augustine states that we won't be able to go seriously off track if we have internalized Christ and are living in Christ's Spirit. We will not be capable of giving ourselves over to lavish living, exploitation of the poor, abuse of children, drunken orgies, or rape of the land if we love God.

We won't propagate an anything-goes morality that makes a mockery of industry, family life, childbearing, and the disadvantaged.

Apparently, off-color and off-track behaviors were afflicting the community Jude was addressing. He had to caution them that Christian freedom is not unfettered. It isn't license and licentiousness.

Jude was sure that faithful prayer and the remembrance of mercy would not stand for a gospel of Anything Goes. The Holy Spirit could not countenance a Whatever-Floats-Your-Boat ethic displacing the genuine Good News. That would be, then and now, anti-Word.

≡ PRAYER

Spirit of God, help me and all of us remember that virtue is definite and distinct. We're not called to be straitjacketed, but we know that Christ told us we would be on a narrow road. Let me, let us, be joyfully sensuous but never outrageously sensual. Some things do offend you.

≡ FOR REFLECTION

- Christians are cautioned to be on guard against false teachings. What are some of the predominant ones of our day? How do we know?

- How do we account for the fact that some religious people, even those ministering in the church, sometimes go seriously off track and become, for all intents and purposes, more hedonist than evangelist? What seems to have driven (or maybe seduced) them?

⇒ **READ REVELATION 22**

The Spirit and the bride say, "Come." REVELATION 22:17

The church is missionary, and so, by virtue of baptism, is every Christian. Cardinal Avery Dulles has spoken of the church's "twofold mission of the Word and the Spirit" (Dulles, 116). That double mission is all about the transformation of the world. Thus, it is our mission to leave the world a better place, a more loving and reverent place, for our having been here.

All the apocalyptic imagery of the Book of Revelation has led believers for centuries and even millennia to try to calculate the timing of the cataclysm that would set loose four horsemen and stoke the final battle. The New Jerusalem they envision has some very nice characteristics of planet Earth but is apparently elsewhere. Christ the King and hordes of angels descend, but the gist of the story seems to be that we're swept away to somewhere beyond our galaxy.

But there's a little what-if to consider. Let us suppose that we do substantially succeed in transforming the earth in a positive direction.

Suppose that we work out ways for the rich to divide their spoils lavishly with the poor. Suppose that famine and disease-ridden countries have a green revolution, provide superb medical care for everyone, and enact means to squelch any and all traces of political corruption. Suppose that terrorists and criminals are converted and that the gun lobby decides to invest energy in rose gardens instead. Suppose that education is universally available and that billions are adequately trained for meaningful work. Suppose that hours of work and leisure are balanced and that vowed or contracted commitments are kept. Suppose that truth-telling becomes normative and that all human societies support life from conception until natural death.

Clearly a universal conversion to God and the good does not seem likely, but decisive steps in that direction could be taken. Prayer, fasting, and almsgiving can extend beyond the paltry effects of Lent and Yom Kippur and Ramadan. These three classic disciplines can lift great weights. If they finally do, the old Holy Land and the global metropolises might look considerably more like the New Jerusalem.

There are more than a few hints in the gospels that the reign of God, the realm of God, is in our midst and meant for the here and now, not just some far off place and much later.

When the Spirit and the bride, the people of God, say "Come," it certainly bears the tones of invitation directed to where we are and when we are. If we breathe in the Spirit and breathe out the love we've received, perhaps we can help leverage the promised end-time to a seamless new beginning. A chapter earlier, the Spirit-inspired last book of the Bible describes what that might be like:

> Then I saw a new heaven and a new earth…See, the home of
> God is among mortals. He will dwell with them as their God;
> they will be his peoples, and God himself will be with them;
> he will wipe every tear from their eyes. Death will be no more;
> mourning and crying and pain will be no more, for the first
> things have passed away. REVELATION 21:1, 3–4

The Spirit is always and everywhere about awakening to creative, beneficent, holy possibility. The mission for us who revere the word and do our best to live a Spirit-led life is to help that possibility become vibrantly, richly, dazzlingly alive.

Help me, Spirit of God and Lord of Life, to do whatever I can to fulfill the double mission you send. Help me in some way to jump-start the Alpha-and-Omega future to which you call us. Really.

≣ **FOR REFLECTION**

- When I think of the end of the world, what do I envision? Is it a horror story or great homecoming?

- What do I find most puzzling in the Book of Revelation? What parts seem easier to understand?

- The "woman clothed with the sun" in Revelation 12 is very like the familiar image of Our Lady of Guadalupe. What do I believe the role of the Mother of God will be as we move into the final phase of Christian and world history?

AFTERWORD

How do we get the Spirit?

By faith, we believe that we get the Spirit at baptism and get the Spirit's gutsiness strengthened at confirmation.

But how do we really *get* that we've got the Spirit?

Sometimes it seems that it's simply by breathing. When we attend to the aliveness of ourselves, we sometimes break through to awareness that all of planet Earth is alive with life as it rotates steadily and revolves faithfully around the sun.

We get the Spirit by desiring. Dominican Father Donald Goergen quotes a prayer of St. Symeon the New Theologian that invokes the Holy Spirit nobly as "You who have become desire Yourself in me, who have made me desire You" (Goergen, 177). In other words, the saint sees the Spirit as the one who implants holy desire in us, such that when we desire holy and wholesome things, we desire in the Spirit. Doing so, we desire the Spirit in person.

And so sometimes we are inspired. New ideas, discoveries, humanitarian projects, new goals spur us on, and we believe again that our lives matter and that in some small way we can change the world. We speak wisdom that we did not know was ours, and sometimes we are told later that we changed or actually saved a life.

We get the Spirit by letting ourselves be used—for good, for others, for the good earth.

And certainly we get the Spirit, have the Spirit, cherish the Spirit, cling to the Spirit when we love. By nature and by grace, we're called to family, friendship, coworking, and community. We're drawn, heart to heart, soul to soul, by the Spirit.

St. Basil the Great, writing in the fourth century, says it this way:

> When a ray of light falls upon clear and translucent bodies,
> they are themselves filled with light and gleam with light from
> within themselves. Just so are the Spirit-bearing souls that
> are illuminated by the Holy Spirit. They are themselves made
> spiritual, and they send forth grace to others. ST. BASIL, 54

It is when we love that we radiate God from within. We spill over with goodness, achieve "heavenly citizenship," and are actually "becoming God," says Basil. The Eastern fathers call this *theosis* or divinization, becoming overtaken by godliness.

When we love magnificently, we really get the Spirit. But the Spirit is never wholly gotten. So our purpose and passion require willful perseverance.

That's why we always need to study, always need to listen and learn, and always, always need to pray—with inner confidence and undying joy.

FOR FURTHER READING

Many of the works that follow are cited in this text. Some are more devotional. Some are intended for slow pondering. Some (especially Congar) focus on the theology of the Spirit.

Apostoli, Fr. Andrew, CFR. *Paraclete: The Spirit of Truth in the Church*. Cincinnati: Servant Books, 2005.

Caster, Fr. Gary. *Inspired: The Powerful Presence of the Holy Spirit*. Cincinnati: Servant Books, 2015.

Catechism of the Catholic Church, Second Edition. Washington: United States Catholic Conference, 1997. Especially see Part One, Article 8; Part Two, Article 2; Part Three, Article 7.

Congar, Yves. *I Believe in the Holy Spirit*, trans. David Smith. New York: Crossroad Publishing, 1983.

Donnelly, Doris, ed. *Retrieving Charisms for the Twenty-First Century*. Collegeville, MN: Liturgical Press, 1999.

Dulles, Avery, SJ. *The New World of Faith*. Huntington, IN: Our Sunday Visitor Publishing, 2000.

Estrada, Hugo. *Espiritu Santo en la Biblia y en Nuestro Vida*. Santafe de Bogota, Colombia: San Pablo, 1997.

Goergen, Donald J., OP. *Fire of Love: Encountering the Holy Spirit*. New York: Paulist Press, 2006.

Hensell, Eugene, OSB. "Scripture Scope: Why Read the Biblical Prophets Today," *Review for Religious* 70 (2011): 323.

John Paul II. *On the Holy Spirit in the Life of the Church and the World (Dominum et Vivificantem)*, Vatican trans. Boston: Daughters of St. Paul, 1986.

Liguori, St. Alphonsus, "Novena to the Holy Spirit," in Norman J. Muckerman, CSsR, ed. *From the Heart of St. Alphonsus: Favorite Devotions from the Doctor of Prayer*. Liguori, MO: Liguori Publications, 2002.

Martinez, Archbishop Luis M. *The Sanctifier*, trans. Sister M. Aquinas, OSU. Boston: Pauline Books and Media, 2003.

—. *True Devotion to the Holy Spirit*, trans. Sister M. Aquinas, OSU. Manchester, NH: Sophia Institute Press, 2000.

Moore, Brian, SJ. *Devotions to the Holy Spirit*. Boston: Pauline Books and Media, 1988 (American edition).

Spurgeon, Charles. *Holy Spirit Power*. New Kensington, PA: Whitaker House, 1996.

St. Basil the Great. *On the Holy Spirit*, trans. and intro. Stephen Hildebrand. Yonkers: St. Vladimir's Seminary Press, 2011.

Underhill, Evelyn. *The Life of the Spirit, the Life of Today*. Harrisburg, PA: Morehouse Publishing, 1994; reprint from London: Methuen, 1922.

Wolf, Alexys S. *Holy Spirit Who: Discovering and Getting to Know the Person of the Holy Spirit*. Lexington, SC: Xlibris Publishing (e-book), in conjunction with Fiery Sword Global Ministries, 2011.